In the name of God, most Gracious, most Merciful

THE DAY
OF
RISING

Laila Mabruk

Dar Al-Taqwa

© Dar Al Taqwa Ltd. 1997

ISBN 1 870582 85 3

Translation: Aisha Bewley

Editors: Abdalhaqq Bewley and Muhammad Isa Waley

Production: Bookwork, Norwich

Published by:
    Dar Al Taqwa Ltd.
    7A Melcombe Street
    Baker Street
    London NW1 6AE

Printed and Bound by- De-Luxe Printers,
London NW10 7NR.
website: http://www.de-luxe.com
email: naresh@aapi.co.uk

In the name of Allah, the Merciful, the Compassionate

*"The Day they issue forth and not one
thing about them will be hidden from
Allah. 'To whom does sovereignty
belong today?' 'To Allah, the One, the
Conqueror. Today every soul shall be
repaid for what it earned. There will no
wronging today. Allah is swift at the
Reckoning.'"* (40:16-17)

Table of Contents

Introduction

*"O my people, the life of this world is but fleeting
enjoyment. The Next World is the Abode
of Permanent Residence." (40:39)*

We began this journey in our small book, *The Soul's Journey
after Death*. In that book we dealt with the lesser Last Hour, the
moment a person dies, the instant the soul leaves the body. We
described the way the soul moves to another world; how it meets
with other souls; how it sees, hears and speaks using other sensory
faculties; how it connects with its earthly body and feels bliss or
punishment. That book was translated into English in London and
has been published more than once in Arabic.

Then we moved on to the second stage of the journey in a book
entitled *The Book of the Last Day* in which we investigated numerous topics, all of which concern the Last Day, the moment of the
death of this world which presages our journey to the Next. We
mentioned the lesser and greater signs of the Last Day which
include signs which have come and gone and others which have
appeared and are still going on and will continue to do so until the
end of time. There are major signs indicating the imminent
approach of the Last Day and others indicating its imminent
arrival. We dealt with the question of what Existence was before
its creation and how it will cease to exist at the end of time, con-
sidering existence from a number of different angles. We reflected
on the scientific insights which the Qur'an was the first to present
and which have now been corroborated by many scientists.

We will all experience the Last Day when the Trumpet will be
sounded. The first blast will terrify all creatures and end by their

becoming unconscious. Everything in the heavens and the earth will lose consciousness.

> *"There was but one Great Shout and they were deathly still."* (36:29)

Heaven will envelop the earth and nothing will remain except Allah, the One, the Conqueror, Who has existed from before time began and will continue to exist after time comes to an end.

> *"Do not call on another god with Allah. There is no god but Him. All things are perishing except His Face. His is the judgement and to Him you will be returned."* (28:88)

This, the third book in the series, concerns the Day of Rising which will begin with the second Trumpet Blast: the Blast of Resurrection when humanity will be resurrected in another world completely different from this limited world which we inhabit now. They will be transported, spirit and body, from the ephemeral life of this world to the everlasting timelessnessness of the Next World. The Scales will be set up and justice will prevail, or rather that vast Divine Mercy which precedes justice will prevail. The Almighty says:

> *"Say: 'To whom does everything in the heavens and earth belong?' Say: 'To Allah. He has made mercy incumbent upon Himself. He will gather you to the Day of Rising about which there is no doubt. As for those who have lost their own selves, they do not believe."* (6:12)

The Reckoning will begin and the hateful elements of evil will be singled out for the Blaze of Hellfire and the forces of good will win the Garden of Delight. That is how the Day of Rising will end. It is the Day of Reckoning, the time of repayment for all our deeds. This is the subject of the final instalment of the series *The Journey to the Eternal World*. If Allah has so decreed, I will accompany you, my fellow human being, so that we complete our

4

journey together to the Delights of the Gardens of Paradise, casting a glance at the Hellfire on the way. Then you will see whether or not the Lord of Might is generous to us.

You can read each book of the series as a book on its own or you can read them together as links in the chain of the journey to the Eternal World. Read them however you wish. The important thing is for you to know what they contain so that you can prepare yourself and do everything you can to save yourself from the punishment of the Next World and win its timeless bliss.

You should know that the Next World with all its particulars and the order of its events is in reality known only to Allah; and that what I write represents merely a few features in the landscape of that immeasurable World. Those features are what the Almighty has allowed us to know by presenting them to us in His Noble Book and on the tongue of His Noble Prophet and which have therefore become necessary for every human being to know.

In talking of it I will refer to the Noble Qur'an, about which there is no dispute, and also to the noble *hadiths*, attempting to to be very careful to select only those which are sound. I will also consult the *tafsirs* of trustworthy scholars past and present and compare the *tafsirs* of the scholars of different times in order to reach the most appropriate explanation of the *ayats* of Allah and the *hadiths* of the Messenger of Allah, may Allah bless him and grant him peace. Finally I will attempt to present this information in a style which makes it accessible to the greatest number of people. I pray to Allah to grant me success in all that contains good and is pleasing to Him and to keep me far from anything that contains evil and is hateful to Him.

"Do not imagine that Allah will break His promise to His Messengers. Allah is Almighty, Exactor of Revenge. On the day the earth is changed to other than the earth, and the heavens likewise, and they parade before Allah, the One, the Conquering, you will see the evildoers that Day yoked together in chains, wearing shirts of tar, their faces enveloped in the Fire so that Allah can repay every self for what it earned. Allah is Swift at Reckoning. This is

5

a communication to be conveyed to mankind so that they may be warned by it and so that they may know that He is One God, and so that people of intelligence will remember." (14:48-52)

This World Compared
to the Next World[1]

"Are you happier with the life of this world than with the Next? Yet the enjoyment of the life of this world compared to the Next World is very small." (9:38)

The human creature is indeed an enigma! When this world smiles on us we imagine that it is ours completely and that we are going to live for ever. We imagine it to be the Garden of Paradise and our overriding preoccupation becomes enjoying its pleasures as much as we possibly can. We do our best to forget the Next World and neglect it, clinging to optimism and refusing to be pessimistic about it. But at the same time we flee from the very idea of the Day of Rising because it inevitably entails terror, alarm and fear.

On the other hand, when this world makes us weep we feel it as a constricting burden and imagine it to be the very Blaze of Hellfire. We become filled with anxiety and fear and that leads some people to seek escape from it, even by suicide. Such people do not take account of what follows suicide. They do not realise that they are fleeing from a transient, insignificant pain only to be confronted by the inescapable agony of eternal punishment.

It is a mystery why a sensation of pessimism and depression should make the idea of death attractive to people to such an extent that they lose sight of the Next World and suspect it of

1. Ibn Mas'ud narrated that the Messenger, may Allah bless him and grant him peace, said: "What have I do with this world? In this world I am only like a rider who pauses for shade under a tree and then travels on and leaves it." (related by at-Tirmidhi)

7

being illusory, claiming that only this world is real. You have misjudged the situation badly if you think that fears and worries about this world are of greater import than concern for the Next World.

"But you prefer the life of this world even though the Next World is better and longer lasting." (87:16-17)

However, there is no reason not to look on the bright side of death and the Next World. Is it not true that the grave can be a place of bliss as well as of punishment, that on the Day of Rising there will be mercy, justice and fairness as well as alarm, over-whelming force and terror? On the Day of Rising mercy will take precedence, then justice, and only in the last resort force against those who rebelled or rejected. Do we not repeat in the *Fatiha* in every prayer and before every *sura* of the Qur'an, *"In the name of Allah the All-Merciful, the Most Merciful"*? If we look at the two words, "All-Merciful, Most Merciful," we find that the attribute of mercy is manifested in them in the deepest and most complete and intensive way, it being the foremost of Allah's attributes.

How is it possible for us to be pessimistic about the Day of Rising after this, once we know that it is under the control of the Lord of the Worlds, the "Most Merciful of the Merciful", the "All-Merciful, Most Merciful"? How can we have a bad opinion of Allah – glory be to Him and may He be exalted – when He says in a *hadith qudsi*, "I am in My slave's opinion of Me" (Al-Bukhari, Muslim, at-Tirmidhi and Ibn Majah, from Abu Hurayra)? We should indeed have a good opinion of Allah. Whose mercy encompasses everything so that it takes precedence over His justice.

"Those who come with a good action will have ten like it. Those who come with a bad action will only be repaid the same as it and they will not be wronged." (6:160)

"Allah does not wrong anyone by even the tiniest speck. And if there is a good deed Allah will multiply it and pay out an enormous wage direct from Him." (4:40)

8

If mercy comes before justice, it is even further in advance of wrath and violent force. According to a *hadith qudsi* transmitted by al-Bukhari, when Allah finished creating creation, written in His Presence above His Throne were the words, "My mercy comes before My wrath." (Also in Muslim and Ibn Majah)

Being overcome by the terrors and concerns of this world only leads to despair and disappointment in both this world and the Next. If we reflect on the *ayats* of Allah Almighty, we will replace this sensation of gloom with other feelings overflowing with love and optimism regarding the Next World and this world which will lead us automatically to prayer and the constant performance in this world of all those things which bring us near to Allah, things which contain the good of both this world and the Next.

In *Surat al-Baqara,* the first *sura* of the Qur'an after the *Fatiha*, we find that the first *ayats* list the attributes of the godfearing. The first of them is belief in the Unseen; the last is complete certainty regarding the Next World, which is the highest degree of faith.

> *"Alif - Lam - Mim. That is the Book with no doubt. In it is guidance for the godfearing: those who believe in the Unseen and establish the prayer and give of what We have provided for them; who believe in what has been sent down to you and what was sent down before you, and are certain of the Next World."* (2:1-4)

He did not simply say, "they believe". Faith in Allah, His Books, His Messengers, His angels, His decree of good and evil and the Last Day and other matters of this world and the Next which are invisible to us but which are brought together by the term "the Unseen" must permeate us completely so that our actions are governed by it and so that while we enjoy this world we at the same time cultivate it in order to win the Next World:

> *"The life of this world is nothing but a game and a diversion. The abode of the Next World, truly that is Life, if they only knew."* (29:64)

9

This world is a mixture of transient joys and sorrows which only represent faint intimations of the bliss and punishment of the Next World. The tomorrow of this world may never arrive and it will be seen to have been an illusion. But the tomorrow of the Next World is a reality which cannot be avoided. That is what we should strive for and our efforts must be based on the study of the many *ayats* of the Qur'an relating to this subject and what has been related about it from the Prophet, may Allah bless him and grant him peace. Striving does not mean complete asceticism in this world and giving up everything for the Next World, for the true gauge of success in this world and winning the Next World is action in this world and enjoying the blessings of Allah in it and being steadfast in the face of its afflictions.

"Seek, in respect of what Allah has given you, the abode of the Next World, not forgetting your portion of this world..." (28:77)

There is a great difference between acting in this world for the sake of this world and acting in this world for the sake of the Next World. Action for the sake of this world alone is the result of a superficial and narrow perspective which confines the human being within the bounds of this limited dimension of existence and leads to a fruitless struggle for possessions and position and an excessive concern with worldly sorrows and joys. It also encourages characteristics which we can well do without, such as rancour and hypocrisy.

Acting for the sake of the Next World, on the other hand, demands deep insight and an intellect open to both this world and the Next, and leads to mutual cooperation in gaining the best from this world out of desire for the Next and to moderation in respect of its joys and sorrows. By its nature it encourages characteristics of which we are mostly in great need such as truthfulness and sincerity.

It is vital for us to keep this world in the correct perspective both in respect of its sweet and bitter aspects and not to inflate its importance beyond its deserts. We should not be extravagant in our feelings about it nor should we deny them completely; we should not go to excess in either sorrow or joy; be happy and sad but in measure. We must remember that this world is neither Paradise nor Hellfire, merely an extremely faint and limited foretaste of the joys of the one and the torment of the other. In this world both good and evil people taste a mixture of delight and punishment together. In the Next World immeasurable delight is for the good alone and endless punishment for the evil. This world is a tiny drop compared to the vast ocean of the Next World.[1]

This world: a mixture of good and evil

In this world good and evil are mixed together, conflicting and interlocking with one another. Life with its inherent beauty is naturally and fundamentally good. Evil is created alongside it in this world as a means of instruction and as an affliction to put us to the test. This world is like a primary school devoted to instruction and teaching where we take an entrance examination for the Next World. All who pass will become a force for good and obtain the bliss of the Next World. Those who fail become an instrument of evil and bring on themselves the punishment of the Next World.

Life is basically good and for good, but the immense forces of good cannot fully dominate in the life of this world because of the inevitable struggle against the hateful forces of evil. Because this world exists merely to sift out the good from the bad, it will remain only as long as good remains and it will end once all good has departed. When only evil remains and no good is present to combat it, evil will turn against itself and the end will come and the Last Day arrive. The ephemeral life of this world will end with the transferral of all life to the Next World.

---

1. In *Fath al-Bari*, a commentary on the *Sahih* of al-Bukhari, pt. 11; Muslim, at-Tirmidhi and an-Nasa'i transmitted by way of Qays ibn Abi Hazim from al-Mustawrid ibn Shaddad, "By Allah, this world in relation to the Next World is only like someone dipping his finger in the sea. Let him see the amount he brings out [compared to the immensity of the sea]."

The Next World: the separation of good and evil

The Day of Rising is also the Day of Reckoning, a very precise reckoning in which justice will prevail. Justice demands that the forces of good be distinguished from the forces of evil and that repayment take place. Since life is basically good and for good, the people of good – the people of wholesomeness, love, and justice – will live in the company of wealth and beauty in the Garden of Bliss. The people of evil – the people of evil, hatred, and injustice – will end up with poverty, ugliness and punishment in Hellfire. The forces of good are magnified exponentially once they are separated from the forces of evil and so ultimate perfect enjoyment without any limit is only possible in the life of the Next World, far removed from all evil. Thus the life of the Next World will remain as absolute good forever. The opposite applies to with the forces of evil.

> "So that Allah may sift the bad out from the good, and pile the bad on top of one another, heaping them all together, and cast them into Jahannam. They are the losers." (8:37)

A story from real life

What happens, though, when good and evil meet? Before answering this question, I would like to tell you a story. It is something that actually happened and will explain much of what I want to say on this subject. See it in terms of general human experience set within the framework of a particular situation experienced by one individual. It is a story about a group of friends of whom I was one and in particular about a girl called Samiyya who was also one of us.

Samiyya was the flower of our group, a bundle of vitality and energy, a noble generous human being, bursting with love of people and love of good. Her optimism and love of life were unbounded. She was a loving person, sweet and unaffected. You would have loved her jokes and even her rare moments of petulance. You would have loved her a lot.

Time passed and circumstances changed. Samiyya became ill. But although she was ill her constant energy remained unabated. The doctors could not tell her what was wrong. She began to fear the future and she became obsessed with the idea of death. She would say, "I dreamt that I was going to die." I could hear the undertone of sorrow and deep grief in her voice as she said this but she quickly returned to her jokes and customary laughter and inexhaustible sweetness. She did not let on that she was ill except by an odd word uttered here and there among all the jokes and laughter, and all of us thought she was imagining things. Then one day Samiyya stayed in bed; she was unable to move for several days, and she was taken to hospital.

It finally became clear that she was indeed very ill and within a very short time Samiyya died. She died in the full bloom of her youth and at the peak of her vitality. With her death the brightest light of my life went out. The world became a dark and narrow place which I hated. I could not imagine life without Samiyya. I thought my tears would never stop flowing and that my life had had lost all point. I thought about death and began to hate it and fear the Next World. Deep sorrow overwhelmed me. I became filled with anxiety, as did we all. We only knew that a beautiful flower had been plucked suddenly from our midst. We were overcome by despondency.

As time passed, however, and we gradually began to smile again, I submitted to reality, to the finality of the Decree which is stronger than any human being, and began to live again. I decided to make a truce with death and the Next World and with the Decree in general. So I read and learned and finally wrote. Layla, who was another of the friends in our group, read what I wrote. I will never forget the day she said to me after reading my book, "Although it is a book about death and the Next World, your style made me read it with a smile." Allah! What sweet words! "A book about death" and "I read it with a smile." I can still hear her saying this: a gift from a beloved friend, a fine and gentle human being. Her smile was full of serenity and composure. She was love and

13

kindness itself, even though she was a person of few words. She showed the fineness of her feelings by her noble behaviour. She was the cornerstone of our group.

About a year and a half after Samiyya's death, Layla too became ill. She consulted doctors. She travelled abroad for treatment and returned. She had the best doctors, was surrounded with first-rate medical attention, but no medicine or treatment could do anything for her. She had the same terrible illness as Samiyya, but in an even more severe form. Layla was a chemist and she asked her brother, a doctor, not to tell her what her illness was. She also asked for the label on her medicine bottle to be changed before he gave it to her. She did not want to know the name of the medicine because that would let her know what her illness was. She would say, "What I have is anaemia." Did she really not know the nature of her illness or did she just want to to avoid confronting it? Does the thought of death alarm a human being that much?

Her illness was long and the pain unbearable but Layla bore it, and bore it with courage and fortitude. She did not weep. She did not complain at all in spite of the fact that she was unable to move. I remember I saw her one day with her back in a very painful position. She could not sit up or lie down in a natural position for restful sleep. She was forced to prop herself up somewhere between the two. Her face appeared haggard and pinched owing to the severity of the illness, as if black circles had spread round her eyes until they almost filled her cheeks. In the flood of pain which she often could not conceal, I saw that her eyes were filled with tears. She said, "Leave me," with her usual calm when the pain became severe. "Do you want to hear the Symphony of 'Oh!'?"

The word "Oh!" came from the very depths of her heart and made me as well say to myself, "Oh!" then a thousand more 'Ohs!'. I left her room weeping in order to regain my composure. Layla only gave vent to her pain with a few words, "Oh!... O Lord! ...Praise be to Allah!"

On the Thursday our group of friends met in my house. We read the Noble Qur'an for her, reciting it right through from beginnning to end. We prayed to Allah for healing for her. On the

14

Friday morning the pain went away and it seemed as if a remission was taking place. She was in a confused state. She said to her mother, "Why are you weeping, mother? I have been cured. I am getting better." Then she said, "Where am I?" Her mother replied, "You are at home in bed." She said, "No, I am walking in a beautiful garden."

The following day fate decreed that I should visit her when her consciousness was completely gone and she could not speak. Her breath was only coming with great difficulty. Hours passed and very very slowly her breath became shallower and her eyes opened as if she was staring above her into infinity. It was as if she was wandering in another domain. Then we heard the *adhan* for *'Isha'* which blessed the place; the black circles on her face grew fainter and fainter and her tension eased and all signs of fatigue disappeared. All we could see was a face calm and at peace. We were certain that there were angels present. Hanna' closed the door to keep any sound from entering which might disturb Layla in those solemn final moments. We wanted her to leave us in peace and security. We opened the Qur'an and recited the *Suras Yasin, al-Mulk,* and *ar-Rahman.* When we finished we quietly pronounced the *shahada* and bade her farewell with peace.

Layla had left our world. I felt as if a delicate soul had flown from its house. Released from her physical prison, she had returned home free and liberated to a vast and spacious world. Her trial was over. She had become free from the tribulations of this world to be greeted by the bliss of the Next World. I saw Layla's body when her soul had left it, and I looked at her face. It was as if it was encircled by a halo of light. A sensation of contentment and peace enfolded me. I was certain in my heart about what the Almighty means when He says: *"O soul at rest and at peace! Return to your Lord, well-pleased and well-pleasing."* (89:27-28) Due to that experience I came to love these two *ayats* more and knew what they meant in respect of the Layla who had travelled to the Next World – and also in respect of the Layla, myself, who remains in this one.

"No misfortune occurs except by the permission of Allah. Anyone who believes in Allah, He will guide his heart. Allah has knowledge of all things." (64:11)

Hanna', one of Layla's closest friends, was bewildered and asked, "Why did the Almighty torture her when she was like a faultless angel?" After some days the answer came. Hanna' said, "Last night I dreamt of Layla. She was wearing a beautiful robe, extremely clean and white. Her hair was wet as if she had just come from the bath. Around her I saw palaces and splendid gardens. She said, 'This all belongs to me. They visit me but I am alone.'"

When I heard this I was flooded with joy. I said to Hanna', "I believe, and Allah knows best, that her cleanness and wet hair is a sign of her purification. The torment she endured in this world with patience[1] and thankfulness to Allah was a bath which washed away all her sins. Because of this she has been spared the punishment of the Interspace which purifies Muslims from the impurity of their sins before they can enter the Garden. Layla has already won a state of bliss by Allah's permission. That is indicated by the palaces and beautiful gardens around her. As for her words, 'They visit me, but I am alone,' although all knowledge is with the the the All-Merciful, I believe that those who visit her are the angels and the souls of the deceased Muslims, but she is alone because she was the first of her family and close friends to travel to that world. That indicates that her bliss is not yet complete because she is held in the bliss of the Interspace. Perfect bliss is only experienced in the Garden after the Resurrection and the Reckoning."

---

1. In *Fath al-Bari*, a commentary on the *Sahih al-Bukhari*, v. 10, Muslim transmitted that Suhayb reported that the Messenger of Allah, may Allah bless him and grant him peace, said, "How extraordinary is the situation of the believer! His destiny is all goodness. No one else can claim that. If good fortune comes to the believer, he thanks Allah and has a reward. If harm befalls him, he is steadfast and has a reward. Everything Allah decrees is good for the Muslim." This is further corroborated by the *hadith* from Sa'd ibn Abi Waqqas, "I am astonished at Allah's decree for the believer. If good befalls him, he praises and is thankful. If misfortune befalls him, he praises and is steadfast. The believer is rewarded for everything that happens to him." (Ahmad and an-Nasa'i)

Muhammad ibn Khalid related from his father from his grandfather who was a Companion, "I heard the Messenger of Allah, may Allah bless him and grant

That is our story. I have written it with tears and smiles. I do not mean tears of sorrow, but tears from the feelings provoked by the memory. My smile is one of peace of mind and pleasure at the command of my Lord, the Ever-Compassionate and All-Merciful.

Commentary

Behind every event in life there is a lesson of far-reaching wisdom from the Creator. The important thing is for us to reflect on what happens so that perhaps we may understand it and be able to take a sound position with regard to it. We will then pass our test successfully. The positions people take in the face of what happens to them vary a great deal. Our position in relation to the same occurrence happening more than once can also vary as can be seen from the story I have just told. One friend died and then after that another friend died, but although my love for each of them was overwhelming my reaction was completely different in each instance. Why should this have been the case?

Before Samiyya's death I only had a superficial understanding of death and the Next World gained through reading and hearsay. After her death, I discovered that that is not enough – reading and learning are merely a step on the path. True knowledge can only be developed through stages and disciplining the self. When Samiyya died, I became depressed about life in general. I looked at this limited world in a pessimistic way because my view of the limitless Next World was also basically pessimistic. My actual feeling about death was very different from what my intellect knew of it. I felt it as a real separation. I could see only the grave, darkness, maggots, and a world of unknown terrors. The result was excessive sorrow and despair.

That is the case with most people when they face such a situation. It is due to their ignorance of death and the Next World and

---

him peace, say, 'When a person has a prior station from Allah and does not reach it through his actions, then Allah will test him through his body or children or property. Then he is steadfast in that until he reaches that station." (Ahmad ibn Hanbal and Abu Dawud) their aversion to even thinking about it. They are absorbed by their immediate world which will soon disappear. They invest all their thoughts and hopes in this world and always seek to turn it into a paradise even though that is impossible. They are agitated and anxious. Their sorrow is excessive when they experience the afflictions of this world just as their joy is excessive at its delights. That is because their thoughts are totally centred on it. They become toys in the hands of Shaytan and do not posssess anything for themselves.

When Layla died I could have lost my self-control again and become a toy in the hands of Shaytan; but I had read deeply and more importantly I had written, which meant that I had used both my mind and my heart. I had fully grasped that this world is truly not the only world, that it is only a transient world to which mankind descended as a result of our weakness in the face of Shaytan's trickery. We are here because of an error and the result of that error is a constant struggle between good and evil which is like a test in this transient lesser world. If we are successful in it and defeat Shaytan we will regain our true inheritance for all eternity, far from Shaytan. Otherwise we will descend with Shaytan to the lowest of the low. Our salvation lies in being steadfast under the trials we face in this world. The Almighty says:

> "We will test you with a certain amount of fear and hunger and loss of wealth and life and fruits. But give good news to the steadfast: those who, when disaster strikes them, say, 'Truly we belong to Allah and we shall return to Him.' Those are the ones who have blessings and mercy from their Lord. It is they who are guided."
>
> (2:155-157)

When Layla died I found that I did not love or fear the loss of this ephemeral world: on the contrary, I yearned for the everlasting reward of the Next World. In this way I solved the riddle of death. I began to look to what is beyond this world with a look that was full of love and optimism, and consequently began to regard this world more optimistically. I was no longer subject to despair and

18

gloom in the face of difficult situations because this world was no longer the focus of my concern. In the Book of Allah we find:

"He said, 'Who despairs of the mercy of his Lord except for misguided people?'" (15:56)

When Layla died I realised that although it cannot be denied that death is a terrifying prospect and that sorrow at someone's death is natural, no matter whether it be for the person themselves or at being parted from them, nevertheless there is no need at all for excessive sorrow. Death is not a separation forever, as I used to imagine. It is simply a journey from the Abode of Testing to the Abode of Abiding. Layla travelled as Samiyya had travelled before her. I too will certainly join them on a day which only Allah knows. Then, Allah willing, we will find ourselves far from sorrow in a world which is composed entirely of joys, joys which will never end.

So why should I feel excessive grief for Layla who has gone on? She has been delivered from the torment of this world and transferred to the bliss of the Next World by the permission of Allah, as she herself indicated in her stupor and as Hanna' saw in her dream. Why should I be sad for her when she had striven to please Allah Almighty? Why should I be sad when she steadfastly endured the terrible pains of her illness with with a soul which was at peace and thankful? Is it possible for me to love her more than her Creator does, the All-Merciful, the Most Merciful with Whom she now finds herself?

I found that my grief was really only for myself. In the misfortune of death sorrow flows from the depths of the heart for one thing: only for those who remain alive. The dead are distressed and fearful at the moment of death and then they move to the Abode of Truth and learn their fate. The living remain in the abode of affliction facing the tricks of Shaytan. Sometimes we win and sometimes we lose. We do not know what our fate will be:

"Our Lord, pour down steadfastness upon us and take us back to You as Muslims." (7:126)

Good news for those who are steadfast

There is no doubt that many things happen in our lives for which we are not prepared. It is not enough simply to react at the moment and leave it at that. If you were to shed some light on the event and examine it carefully you would find that there was a great deal in it which you did not grasp immediately and which might have caused you to change your life and helped you to live in a better way.

There is nothing we can have that is more beneficial for us in our lives than the quality of steady endurance in the face of affliction: a steadfastness without complaint or grumbling, a "beautiful steadfastness" combined with guidance, peace of mind and acceptance of the command of the All-Powerful, All-Knowing. Steadfastness is the sure path to rescue on the Day of Rising. It is the Key to the Garden. The Almighty says:

> *"We shall test you until We know the true fighters among you and those who are steadfast, and test what is reported of you."* (47:31)

> *"The steadfast will be paid their wages in full without any reckoning."* (39:10)

The two *Sahih* collections transmit that Ibn Abi Rabah said: "Ibn 'Abbas asked me, 'Shall I tell you of a woman who is one of the people of the Garden?' I said, 'Yes, please do.' He said, 'A black woman came to the Prophet, may Allah bless him and grant him peace, and said, "I have fits and uncover myself. Pray for me." He said, "Be patient." She said, "I uncover myself. Pray to Allah that I do not uncover myself." So he prayed for her.'"

Steadfastness in affliction in this world expiates wrong actions. It lightens a man's punishment in the Next World or averts it from him, and may raise his degree of heavenly bliss. In such cases affliction is a blessing and not a punishment. That is sufficiently confirmed for us by what is related about the Prophets and their steadfastness in affliction, which is too well known to need further comment.

20

'A'isha, may Allah be pleased with her, said, "I heard the Messenger of Allah, may Allah bless him and grant him peace, say, 'No believer is pricked by a thorn without Allah granting him a good deed and removing a bad deed from him through it.'" [1]

If we suppose that the average lifespan of a man is about sixty years and the year 365 days, then his age in days is 21,900. If we we round this off to 20,000, leave out the major sins and work on the basis of his only committing one minor sin a day, this means that at the end of his life he will have at least 20,000 small sins. He cannot enter the Garden, however great his good actions, until he has been completely purified of them. So he bears them on his shoulders and back across the *Sirat* until his purification is complete and he has been cleansed of them. Only then will he be able to gain entry into the Garden. However, in His mercy, Allah Almighty has given man an opportunity to be purified of his sins in this world and if not then, in the throes of death and if not then, after death in the Interspace or on the Day of Rising. Allah is able to forgive whomever He wishes among His servants provided that the servant does not owe restitution for an injustice he has perpetrated against a fellow human being.

There is no human being who does not have both good and evil in him. The proportion varies between different people. A good man must have some faults just as an evil man must have some virtues. Because Allah is pleased with those who believe, He purifies them of evil deeds in this world by means of illness or poverty or some sorrow which afflicts them until they are fit to enter the Garden, pure and clean. But when Allah is angry with an unbeliever, He does not punish him until he has received his full due of this

---

1. Muslim and at-Tirmidhi related from Sufyan ibn 'Uyayna that Abu Hurayra said, "When *'Whoever works evil will be requited accordingly,'* (4:123) was revealed, that was hard on the Muslims and the Messenger of Allah, may Allah bless him and grant him peace, told them, 'Take aim and approach. All that befalls a Muslim is expiation, even a thorn which pricks him and a care which distresses him.'"

Ibn Maja transmitted in his *Sunan* from Abu Hurayra that the Prophet, may Allah bless him and grant him peace, visited someone who was ill with Abu Hurayra. The Messenger of Allah said, "Good news! Allah declares, 'It is My fire which I have given power over My believing slave in this world so that that it may replace his portion of the Fire in the Next World.'"

21

world in the form of health, wealth, rank and joys until he is stripped of all his good deeds. Then he meets Allah without any good actions at all and only deserves the punishment of Hellfire in the Next World.

In a *hadith qudsi* it is related that Abu Hurayra, may Allah be pleased with him, stated: "He, peace and blessings be upon him, said, 'Allah Almighty says, "I do not remove any of My slaves from this world, if I desire to forgive him, without eliminating some of his bad actions through illness in his body or diminition in his livelihood or by some sorrow. If any evil deeds still remain, I make his death difficult so that he meets Me with no evil deeds. By My might and majesty, I do not remove any of My slaves, if I do not desire to forgive him, without repaying him for every good deed he has done with health in his body and joy which comes to him and expansion in his provision. If any of his good deeds remain, I make his death easy for him so that he meets Me with no good deed.'"

'Umar ibn al-Khattab, may Allah be pleased with him, once remarked to the Messenger of Allah, may Allah bless him and grant him peace, "Messenger of Allah, Khusraw and Caesar have all that they have, whereas you are the Chosen One of Allah among His creation." The Messenger of Allah, may Allah bless him and grant him peace, who had been reclining, sat up and said, "Are you subject to doubt, son of Khattab? Those people have their good things here and now in the life of this world." (In one variant we find: "Are you not content that they should have this world and we the Next?")[1]

According to the two *Sahih* and other collections the Messenger of Allah, may Allah bless him and grant him peace, said, "Do not eat or drink from gold or silver vessels. They are for them in this world and for us in the Next World."

So be on guard against major acts of disobedience to Allah and then be on guard even more against minor ones. And be a thousand times more careful against doing injustice to others. Allah is able to forgive His slaves, whereas a human being has no power of forgiveness in the Next World. Do not be made anxious by

---

1. Related in the *Tafsir* of Ibn Kathir, vol. 4, p. 127.

the sorrows which visit you and do not look at the joys which come to others. You do not know the wisdom of Allah. Do not try to make this world into a Paradise – and do not imagine that it is Hell either. Put it in its correct perspective and know that it is a tiny mixture of the two. Be steadfast in this transitory world so that you may gain your everlasting reward in the Next World.

"Anything you have been given is only the enjoyment of the life of this world. What is with Allah is better and longer lasting for those who believe and put their trust in their Lord." (42:36)

"The life of this world is nothing but a game and a diversion. The Next World is better for those who are godfearing. Will you not then use your understanding?" (6:32)

What Happens between the Two Blasts

"He is the First and the Last and the Outward and the Inward. He has knowledge of all things." **(57:3)**

When a person dies, his spirit leaves his body. The body is buried in the earth and it is transformed from blood, flesh and bones into earth as it was in the first place. Only one bone remains, the coccyx, which is the last vertebra in the spinal column. It is the thing on which the creation of man is based and from which he will be reconstituted in his second formation on the Day of Resurrection. The Messenger of Allah, may Allah bless him and grant him peace, said, "The earth consumes all of man except the coccyx. He was asked, "What is that like, Messenger of Allah?" He said, "It is like a seed from which you grow." (Ahmad ibn Hanbal, from Sa'id)

As for the spirit, its place is the Interspace which is the region which separates this world from the Next, a place known only to Allah. The spirit can be in bliss or punishment, connected to its body or separate from it, according to a person's actions in this world and in accordance with the will of the All-Merciful. When the Last Hour arrives and the the Blast of Unconsciousness occurs, the bliss or punishment of the Interspace will end and every sensation of the dead will vanish completely. All of existence will be annihilated. The heavens and the earth will be split apart and all creatures will lose consciousness. Everything in existence will be destroyed and return to what it was before time existed. So existence itself will come to an end.

This world will end. It will end because its existence is not essential. Its being is only borrowed from the Real, Unique,

25

Essential Source of all being, the Divine Existence. When Allah willed, this world came into being; and when He wills, it will end and only He will remain, the First Who has been since before time and before Whom nothing was. Only He will remain, the Last Who will remain after time and after Whom nothing will be. He is also the Outward over Whom nothing can be drawn and the Inward within which nothing can be placed. Glory be to You, O Allah! You are the First and the Last Who absorbs every possibility of time, as You are the Outward and the Inward Who contains every possibility of place. You are the One Essential Reality and on You alone and Your will, knowledge and power all existence depends. Allah speaks the truth:

> "All who are on it shall pass away. And the Face of your Lord shall remain, Master of Majesty and Generosity." (55:26-27)

The time between the two Blasts will last as long as only Allah knows. All that we know is that it is forty, but we do not know whether that means forty days or forty months or forty years. Only Allah knows. Al-Bukhari related from Abu Hurayra that the Prophet, may Allah bless him and grant him peace, said, "There are forty between the two Blasts." They asked, "Forty days, Abu Hurayra?" He replied, "I cannot say." They asked, "Forty years?" He replied, "I cannot say." They asked, "Forty months?" He replied, "I cannot say. Everything of the human being will vanish except for the coccyx from which he will be reconstituted."

In the *Sahih* of Muslim Abu Hurayra reports that the Messenger of Allah, may Allah bless him and grant him peace, said, "There are forty between the two Blasts." They asked, "Days?" He replied, "I cannot say." They asked, "Forty months?" He replied, "I cannot say." They asked, "Forty years?" He replied, "I cannot say." He added, "Then water will descend from heaven and they will grow as plants grow."

He said, "The whole of a human being will decay except for the coccyx, and from it creation will be reconstituted on the Day of Rising." (Muslim, from Abu Hurayra)

26

Glory be to Allah! The All-Knowing, the All-Aware, the All-Powerful, the Compeller, Whose power encompasses everything. He creates what He wills however He wills, with means or without means. He commands and all the human body will decay except for the coccyx which is like a seed in the earth and from which man will be created anew. The winds will blow and Allah will gather the dispersed remains of human bodies from the specks of earth. The rain will fall from heaven from under His Throne to the earth. The coccyx will grow, clay will be transformed into flesh, bones and sinews, and the body will be recreated.

> *"He it is Who sends out the winds, bringing advance news of His mercy, so that when they have lifted up the heavy clouds We dispatch them to a dead land and send down water to it, by means of which We bring forth all kinds of fruit. In the same way We shall bring forth the dead. Perhaps then you will remember."* (7:57)

That is how the bodies of human beings will be recreated. It is not like the first formation which took place by means of pregnancy, birth and suckling. The process in the second formation will be that of plants, as with Adam whose body was created from earth at the very beginning of the human story.

> *"Allah caused you to grow out of the earth. Then He returns you into it and will bring you out again."* (71:17-18)

> *"We created you from it and We shall return you to it and We shall bring you forth from it a second time."* (20:55)

The re-creation of the body will be completed in the grave but it will remain dead and without life because the soul will not yet have returned to it. The decisive moment will approach and the Compeller will give the command and bring His angels back to life. He will revive the Throne-bearers and He will revive Israfil. He will give the command and Israfil will take the Trumpet and

27

put it to his mouth. Then He will bring Jibril and Mika'il to life. The Compeller will summon all the human souls and they will be brought. The souls of the believers will be brought radiant with light and the others will be brought dark. He will take them all and put them into the Trumpet. Then He will command Israfil to blow the second Blast – the Blast of the Resurrection.

"The Trumpet will be blown and all in the heavens and all in the earth will lose all consciousness except for whom Allah wills. Then it will be blown a second time and there they will be, standing, looking on." (39:68)

Man – Child of the Earth

"From it We created you, and to it We will return you, and from it We will bring you forth a second time." (20:55)

We were created out of earth. We are nourished from the earth. We live on the earth. We die and go back into the earth. We will be raised up from the earth. And all the while we are on the earth we are incessantly asking questions: "How can our bodies be recreated after they have dissolved into dust and are mixed with other creatures? How is it possible for all of us be raised up together on the Day of Resurrection? How can the Reckoning be carried out on all of Allah's creatures at the same time? How will we all be able to witness the Reckoning of every individual in that fearful standing? How will we bear the full force of the might of the *Malakut* of Allah which Musa was not able to withstand? How, how, how?" There is no end to such 'hows' and they are not answerable in purely empirical terms.

Human power is limited but the Power of Allah is without constraints or limits. So do not think too much. Do not try to apply your mind to these sorts of questions because the Power of Allah is far beyond the comprehension of the limited human intellect. Allah existed before the beginning of time when there was no such thing as man. We had no existence and the Originator brought us into existence. He will recreate us a second time as He has promised us: *"As We originated the first creation so We will bring it back again. It is a promise binding on Us. That is what We shall do."* (21:104)

It is not difficult for human understanding to grasp the logical precept that it is far easier to regenerate the existence of something which was already there than to create it from nothing in the first place. Nothing is difficult for Allah. This is summarised in His words: *"His command when He desires a thing is to say to it, 'Be!' and it is."* (36:82)

The knowledge of Allah is timeless, but He – glory be to Him! – only discloses whatever of His knowledge He wishes at whatever time He wishes. There are secrets contained in Allah's knowledge which have not yet been disclosed. The whole human race already existed in Adam's back at the time he was created. Each of us came from a cell in our father's loins invisible to the naked eye: *"When your Lord took out all their descendants from the loins of the children of Adam ..."* (7:172)

The source of every human being is a minute drop. Every one of these drops represents the whole life of a human being and carries within it all his qualities and all the secrets of his life. The first thing in the formation of every foetus is the base of the spine. The base of the spine, the bottom tip of the final vertebrae, is known as the coccyx. The *hadiths* make it clear that the whole body of man is built up round it during the formation of the foetus. When a human being dies, the body dissolves into the earth and all of it disintegrates except for the coccyx since the formation of the body will occur from it again on the Day of Resurrection by the permission of Allah.

The Messenger of Allah, may Allah bless him and grant him peace, spoke several times concerning this, including what Abu Dawud transmitted in his *Sunan* from Abu Hurayra, "The earth consumes all of the son of Adam except the coccyx. He was created from it and upon it he is built." (Malik, *al-Muwatta'*) The modern science of embryology has made it clear that the coccyx is what remains of the 'primitive streak'[1] and it affects the formation of the foetus in all its stages, especially the nervous system. Then this 'streak' disappears and nothing of it remains except a trace

---

1. The Primitive Streak consists of two parallel longitudinal folds that develop on the epiblast of a chordate embryo at about six and a half days. It forms the notocord, a slender cord of cells which will become the vertebral column. Along the length of the notochord, a series of paired segments (somites) develop which give rise to bone and tissue. At seven days a trough begins to deepen parallel to the notochord. This is the neural groove which becomes the basis of the nervous system.

which is called the coccyx. The *hadiths* about the coccyx are one of the miracles of the Prophet, may Allah bless him and grant him peace, since he stated that the appearance of the coccyx is a basic precondition for the formation of the foetus. Medical ethics forbid carrying out experiments on embryos once the coccyx appears since it is considered the true beginning of the formation of the foetus.

> *"Let man but look what he was created from. He was created from a spurting liquid, issuing between the back-bone and breast-bone."* (86:5-7)

I still continue to say: the knowledge of Allah has secrets not yet disclosed! Some of them will not be disclosed until the Last Hour!

When a human being is born he inherits from his mother all the elements she possesses and the human body is formed from these elements which are sixteen in number and are also elements of the earth. The first and most important are carbon and oxygen and the last is manganese. We live on the surface of the earth, under its care and subject to its gravity. We eat the plants and animals which are nourished by it. We drink its water and breathe its air. Then we die and are buried in it. It becomes our grave and we disintegrate in it and decay, returning to our source. We become earth – earth within the earth – from which in turn another human being is nourished. The cycle continues and will continue until the Last Hour comes and the command of the Originator and Restorer is given: "Be!" and we will once again come into existence.

In essence and form, despite the uniqueness of the human creature, no human being is exactly the same as any other. Each person has an essence completely distinct from all others, from the creation of Adam to the Last Hour. Each of the fingers on one hand of one man is different from all the others, let alone all the fingers of other people! Nobody's fingerprints are the same as anyone else's: *"Does man reckon We will not re-assemble his bones? On the contrary, We are well able to re-shape his fingers."* (75:3-4)

Every man has a particular smell which belongs to no one else, and so a police dog can distinguish one man by his smell among a whole crowd of others. Every man has a voice timbre which no one else has, and so in this respect too each man is completely distinct from every other. Every body has a particular genetic code which does not correspond to that of any other body. When a man is injured, his wounds swiftly knit together by an internal action of his own body. But when a limb from a person is transplanted to someone else, their body may reject it. Often a mother's body will reject her child's kidney and vice versa. The body knows its own limbs by an individual genetic code which differs completely from all others. That code is what brings about acceptance or rejection.

When a man dies and his body dissolves and its elements are mixed with the elements of the earth it becomes new nourishment and it mixes with the bodies of other creatures. That does not prevent Allah from having power over everything. When Allah's command comes on the Day of Rising the elements of every man will re-gather. Indeed, every creature will have the same proportions they had in this world. The soul of each person will be resurrected with the same body and features, the same form and personality. They will be individually resurrected just as they were in this world, that being the way in which they were distinguished from all the other creatures of Allah from the beginning of the world until the Final Hour.

Allah will resurrect us just as we were in this world. But by His power this form will also be in harmony with the life of the Next World. In this world we live and die. In the Next World we will live and never die. In this world our lives are measured by time since we develop from childhood to youth to old age. In the Next World there is no time. We will remain young forever. The senses are weak in this world but in the Next World they will be keen: *"...today your eyesight is sharp."* (50:22) In this world we could not endure the light of the *Malakut* of Allah. Even Musa, peace be upon, was unable to look at Him and lost consciousness. But in their new forms in the Next World the inhabitants of the Garden will be able to enjoy looking at His noble Face. *"Faces on that Day will be radiant, gazing at their Lord."* (75:22-23)

Enchanced senses in the World of Eternity will enable us to have full enjoyment of pure eternal bliss and the full agony of the punishment of Hellfire without dying. We seek refuge with Allah! He will give us a new kind of form which will be able to hear and witness everything on the Day of Rising: *"...That is a Day to which mankind will all be gathered. That is a Day which will be witnessed by everyone."* (11:103) 'Ali ibn Abi Talib, may Allah be pleased with him, was asked, "How is it possible for Allah to judge every human being at the same time?" He replied, "In the same way that He provides for them all at the same time."

There are billions of events occurring at every instant in this world. One person is born and another dies. There are joys here and sorrows there; wars in some lands and peace in others – all at the same moment. Circumstances change and situations are reversed. Provision is allocated by the Provider to all His creation at the same time but creatures cannot perceive that because their faculties are limited and because the earth consists of barriers and distances. Despite that, human knowledge can hear and see certain events through radio and television. If that is within the power of creatures, how much greater must the power of the Creator be!

The earth will split open on the Day of Resurrection and all of Allah's creation will arise and be gathered in the world of causality. Then they will move to the land of the Next World, a land without seas or mountains, a land without any barriers whatsoever, and the reckoning will be completed. It will be completed in a single Day which has no sequel – a long Day, an arduous Day. No creature will be free from worry. All will be brought back and reckoned one by one. The Reckoning will be completed so that all of Allah's creation can see and hear it. And only Allah knows how that will happen.

> *"They say, 'What! When we are bones and crumbled dust, will we then be raised up as a new creation?' Say: 'It would not matter if you were rock or iron or indeed any creation that you think is harder still!' They will ask, 'Who will bring us back again?' Say: 'He who brought you into being in the first place.'"* (17:49-51)

We find in a *hadith qudsi* that Allah said on the tongue of His Messenger:

"Live how you will, you will certainly die;
Love whom you will, you will certainly leave them;
Own what you will, it will return to the earth;
Do what you will, your deeds will go with you."

(Abu Dawud and at-Tayalisi, from Jabir)

The Blast of Resurrection

"The Trumpet will be blown and at once they will be emerging from their graves towards their Lord." (36:51)

The Trumpet will be blown and all the souls will be expelled from it, flying out like a swarm of bees and filling up the space between heaven and earth. Some of them will sparkle with light and others will be dark. The earth will split open so as to allow the bodies to emerge and each soul will be guided to its body and will slip into it. They will infuse them and imbue them with life in an eternal marriage which will never again experience separation since there will be no more death. So every human being will be brought to life in the grave and will rise in alarm at the terror of the sound of the final Trumpet Blast. The earth will boil and erupt from the depths while he is still inside. Suddenly he will hear a voice call from nearby. Allah will command people to gather for presentation before Him:

> *"Listen hard for the Day when the Summoner shall summon from a nearby place. The Day they hear the Shriek in truth. That is the Day of Emergence. It is We who give life and cause to die, and to Us is the journey's end. The Day the earth is split open from around them as they come rushing forth, that is a gathering easy for Us to achieve."* (50:41-44)

The heart of man will be frozen with fear in those awful moments. His covering of injustice, pride and obduracy will be

35

removed and automatically, in his denuded natural form, the unbeliever will seek refuge in his Lord like the believer. They will seek succour from Him, asking for His mercy and forgiveness. They will cry out from the depths of their being, "O Lord, have mercy on us! O Lord, have mercy on us!"

Then there will be noises – terrifying, alarming noises – which reverberate in every place, sounding like a terrible volcano. It is the earth splitting open above them ready to disgorge everything in it. Then all creatures will be thrown up from it – men, jinn, animals, birds, insects and inanimates. The earth will cast out everything inside it all at once and man will suddenly find himself in the midst of a vast ocean of creatures. They will fly about like lost moths unable to find their way, crashing against all of Allah's creatures. They will crowd the surface of the earth. The crush will be unbearable. Creatures will become like a thick cloud in which individuals cannot be distinguished.

> *"Eyes downcast, they will emerge from their graves like swarming locusts, necks outstretched, eyes transfixed rushing headlong to the Summoner. The rejectors will say, 'This is a merciless Day!'"* (54:7-8)

In the midst of the throes of these terrors the mercy of the Lord will descend from Heaven in the form of angels[1] which will fly in every direction, rejoicing, joyous and jubilant. They will impart the most beautiful and sweetest good news in existence. They will go swiftly to the believers – and in a flash they will draw near to them to meet them saying:

> *"Good news for you today of Gardens with rivers flowing beneath them, to be in them timelessly forever. That is the Great Victory."* (57:12)

The believers will be radiant and overjoyed, filled with overbrimming happiness. They will perceive that they have arisen from the dead and moved to the Next World. They will see themselves

---

1. Not all the angels, but only some of them.

as moths fluttering in the Domain of Allah, swimming alone, drowned in love of Allah. They will desire to fly quickly to the bliss of Allah and forget all the injustice and humiliation they experienced in this world which has passed and departed. They will even forget the terror of their present situation. The moment of justice will draw near – the moment of justice, mercy and timeless bliss. The believers will shake the earth of the grave from their heads.

"They will say, "Praise be to Allah Who has removed all sadness from us. Truly our Lord is Forgiving, Thankful." (35:34)

Those words will trouble the ears of the unbelievers. They will repeat in all the confusion and dismay of people who are crushed and bewildered, "What do you mean, 'removed all sadness from us'? What sadness has been removed from us? We are experiencing the harshest and most terrible sorrow! Where are we? We were asleep!"

"They will say, 'Alas for us! Who has raised us from our resting-place?'" (36:52)

The believers will reply immediately:

"This is what the All-Merciful promised. The Messengers were telling the truth." (36:52)

The wrongdoers will mutter, "The promise of the All-Merciful? The Messengers were telling the truth? Is this now the Day of Rising? Were we dead? What is our fate? Is it to be eternal Hellfire? No, impossible!"

The hopes of the dissolute will be dashed. Their memories will return to the distant past, to their life in this world which has ended, and it will seem like something that has just happened. They denied the Messengers. They denied Allah and Allah's Promise. They wronged the believers. How can they meet Allah today? How can they gain the intercession of the Messengers?

How can they be safe from the grievances of the believers? Many questions and thoughts crowd their bewildered minds and they realise that they have no excuses. They will look around in dismay to see if they can find any way to escape.

Then the shaytans will come at them from every side in their true and appalling shapes. They will be tossed into the midst of a terrifying melee of jinn and wild animals and insects. They will cry out in terror but there will be no one to hear. They will call out for help but there will be no one to respond. Only then will they realise that this is the Final Gathering and that those creatures have been completely stripped of their savagery and are abased and humbled like themselves. They will weep and weep in the most bitter possible way:

> *"The Day they do see the angels, there will be no good news that Day for the evildoers. They will say, 'There is an absolute ban.'"* (25:22)

Despite all these fearsome terrors the believers are aware only of pieces of good news which come to them one after another and they will forget the terrible sights which surround them.

> *"The greatest Terror will not afflict them and the angels will welcome them: 'This is your Day, the one that you were promised.'"* (21:103)

Their hearts will be at peace and joy will return to them anew to envelop their entire being, just as regret and anguish will be rekindled in the depths of the wrongdoers.

> *"Allah certainly does not wrong people in any way. Rather it is people who wrong themselves. On the day He gathers them together – when it will seem if they had tarried no more than an hour of a single day – they will recognise one another. Those who denied the meeting with Allah will have lost. They were not guided." (10:44-45)*

> *"Today no soul will be wronged in any way. You will only be repaid for what you did."* (36:54)

People's recognition of one another

People will recognise one another and they will taken by surprise by the Resurrection and the Gathering. They will call to one
another[1] in the midst of the crowd. They will question one another
and answer in confusion as if they had not yet woken up from
sleep. They will think that they have been asleep and dreaming.
Only then will they grasp that they were dead, and that what they
believed to be a dream was in fact the bliss or punishment of the
Interspace. They will think they have spent only an hour in the
grave, not realising that it has been centuries or aeons. This world
will seem almost nothing to them, as if they had lived in it for a
day or even less than a day. They will be aware that the years of
their lives which they wasted in obtaining this world were only a
few instants before the veil fell away.

This world will have ended and on that Day people will only
have the actions they performed in it. The veil will be stripped
from their eyes to reveal that this world was indeed transient and
that the Next World is now in front of them. What have they prepared for it? How will they be able meet their Lord now the
moment of reckoning has arrived? How will they be able to meet
their Lord, before Whom they have now emerged without veil or
cover? The Hour of Reckoning has arrived and they have emerged
with their sins and errors weighing down their backs. What repayment can they expect in this new world of Perpetuity and Eternity?
Questions will press in on their minds from all sides. The blood
will boil in their veins. The weak will call out to the strong.

> *"They will all parade before Allah and the weak will
> say to those who were arrogant, 'We followed you, so can
> you help us at all against the punishment of Allah?' ..."*
> (14:21)

The weak imagine that their weakness will be an excuse for
them and they do not grasp that it is in itself a crime. Incapacity

---

1. The Day of Rising is called the Day of Mutual Calling since people who
were misguided will call to those who led them astray in this world and ask them
to avert the punishment from them.

does not lie in poverty or illness or lack of power. The weakness about which people will be questioned is weakness of the intellect, conscience and will. However much one man controls another he cannot control his intellect, conscience or will unless the other humbles himself voluntarily. Thus people only become weak as a consequence of their thoughts, belief, and conduct. On the Day of Resurrection they will have full responsibility before Allah for any aspect of inner freedom, nobility and humanity they have neglected. The strong will deny any responsibility for the fate of the weak.

> *"They will say, 'If Allah had guided us, we would have guided you. It makes no difference whether we are unable to stand it or we bear it with patience. We have no way of escape."* (14:21)

They will say, "Why are you blaming us? We were not guided and so we misguided you. If Allah had guided us we would have guided you as well. Why are you so anxious about the punishment? Is it conceivable that Allah will show us mercy today after we committed sins which have now become physical burdens on our backs? Linear time has gone and the business is decided. There is no means to escape the punishment." The arrogant will admit the supremacy of the power of Allah which they often used to deny in this world. It is now the Day of Resurrection and they are forced to admit that guidance and misguidance are in Allah's hands alone – Allah Who cannot ever command misguidance.

> *"Allah does not command indecency. Do you say about Allah what you do not know?"* (7:28)

> *"Shaytan promises you poverty and commands you to avarice. Allah promises you forgiveness from Him and abundance. Allah is Boundless, Knowing."* (2:268)

People will criticise one another and will argue about what happened between them.

"On that Day the closest of friends will be enemies to one another, except for the godfearing." (43:67)

The oppressed will put the blame on the tyrants, and the tyrants in turn will blame Shaytan. Shaytan will then blame all of them after appearing clearly among them in his true frightful form. He kept close to them in this world without their eyes being able to see him. He whispered in their breasts. He made disbelief and obduracy attractive to them and seduced them into disobedience, ,and the dissolute followed him. Then on this Day after the end of linear time he will wash his hands of them. Indeed, he will actually blame them for responding to his false call and rejecting the call of Truth from Allah. He will blame them because they followed him in spite of knowing about his ancient enmity towards them. Shaytan will stand among the people after the veil has been lifted from them and will speak out with characteristic audacity and clarity.

"When the matter is decided Shaytan will say, 'Allah made you a promise, a promise of truth, and I made you a promise and broke my promise. I had no authority over you except that I called you, and you responded to me. So do not blame me but blame yourselves. I cannot come to your aid nor you to mine. I reject your having previously made me a partner to Allah.' The wrongdoers shall have a painful punishment." (14:22)

On that Day people will be panic-stricken and the bickering will be intense.

"But then on the Day of Rising you will reject each other and curse each other." (29:25)

Suddenly complete silence will reign. Everyone will stretch out their necks and lift up their eyes, straining to listen. Then a strong, compelling voice will fill all Existence:

"O My slaves! No fear for you today. You will know no sorrow." (43:68)

All creatures will be full of hope and joy will spread across their faces until the conditions are made known.

"Those who believed in Our Signs and submitted themselves." (43:69)

The unbelievers then will be struck down with despair and utter despondency while the hearts of the believers take flight with unparallelled happiness. Their eyes will overflow with tears of joy. They will move quickly, repeating in one voice, with love, respect and great resolve: "There is no god but Allah.[1] There is no god but Allah alone with no partner. His is the kingdom and all praise. He has power over everything."

The bodies of the evildoers will tremble and they will increase in fear and dismay. The unbelievers will bow their heads and their hearts will be filled with regret that they did not accustom themselves to doing so before. A wailing woman will grab the man walking beside her with bowed head, his eyes overflowing with tears. She will cling to him and beseech him, "Tell me, by Allah, why are they shouting?" The man will shriek at her, "Are you still ignorant of the fact that this is the Day of Rising? Do you not perceive the gravity of the affliction which has befallen us!" The woman will be utterly dismayed. She will beat her breast and repeat, muttering in her dismay, "Affliction? The Day of Rising?"

1. In *ad-Dibaj*, it is mentioned that Ibn 'Abbas and 'Ali ibn Husayn reported that the Messenger of Allah, may Allah bless him and grant him peace, said, "Jibril, peace be upon him, told me that the words 'There is no god but Allah' accompany a Muslim when he dies and in his grave and when he leaves his grave. O Muhammad! If you could see them when they rise from their graves shaking the dust from their heads! They will say, 'There is no god but Allah. Praise be to Allah' with radiant faces, but the others will call out, 'Alas for what I neglected in respect to Allah,' with blackened faces."

2. An-Nasa'i related that the Prophet, may Allah bless him and grant him peace, said, "A wailing woman will arise from her grave on the Day of Rising unkempt and dusty, wearing a dress of Allah's curse and a chemise of fire, her hand on her head, saying, 'O woe!' Something similar is transmitted by Muslim and Ibn Majah from Malik al-Ash'ari who reported that the Messenger of Allah,

Then she will slap her face and cry out in a loud voice, striking herself on her head, shrieking, "O my affliction! O my grief! O my woe!"[2]

The rest of the wailers will be alarmed. They will run and repeat the same words behind her with a single voice. The evil will hear that and will be completely shocked and the feeling of terror which entered them will erupt and they will scream: "Alas for us for what we neglected in respect of Allah!"

> "Those who deny the meeting with Allah have lost, so that, when the Hour comes upon them suddenly, they will say, "Alas for the things we neglected there!' They will bear their burdens on their backs. How evil is what they bear!" (6:31)

> "Anyone who misappropriates will arrive on the Day of Rising with what he misappropriated. Then every soul shall be paid in full for what it earned. They will not be wronged. Is one who pursues the pleasure of Allah the same as one who incurs displeasure from Allah and whose refuge is Jahannam? What an evil journey's end! They have different ranks with Allah. Allah sees all that they do." (3:161-163)

The believers, on the other hand, will be jubilant. Anyone who died on *hajj* or *'umra* will be saying, with strength and zeal,[1] "At Your service, O Allah, at Your service! At Your service! You have no partner! At Your service! Praise and blessing is Yours, and the Kingdom. You have no partner."

---

may Allah bless him and grant him peace said, "Wailing is something of the *Jahiliyya*. When the woman wailer dies, Allah will cut garments of fire for her and a chemise from the flames of the fire."

1. Muslim related from Ibn 'Abbas that once a man was in *ihram* with the Messenger of Allah, may Allah bless him and grant him peace, and his camel trampled him and he died. The Messenger of Allah, may Allah bless him and grant him peace, said. 'Wash him with water and lotus and shroud him in his garment. Do not put perfume on him or cover his head. He will be resurrected on the Day of Rising saying the *talbiya*." (al-Bukhari)

43

Everyone who suffered an unjust death with fortitude and humility will call out, full of hope, "Allah is enough for us and the best Guardian. Allah is enough for us and the best Guardian." There will be voices, innumerable voices rising everywhere: this one saying the *takbir*, "Allah is greater!", that one repeating praise and thankfulness; and those who called the *adhan* in this world will be raised calling the *adhan* on the Day of Rising. Everyone will be raised according to how they died. [1]

In spite of the smallness of their numbers, the believers in the midst of this awesome gathering of creatures will be strong and on that Day their voices will rise above the voices of the unbelievers. Their faces will shine with light and be radiant with joy. The faces of the evil will be black with gloom and sorrow:

> *"The Day when faces turn white and faces turn black. As for the people whose faces turn black: 'What! Did you reject after having had belief? Taste the punishment because you rejected!' As for those whose faces turn white, they are in the mercy of Allah, remaining in it timelessly, forever."* (3:106-107)

The blazing sun and oceans of sweat

The good news will bring those who receive it to the front and anguish will move all the others to the rear, but all will be driven along together.

> *"Every soul shall come together with a driver and a witness."* (50:21)

An angel will go behind every person to drive him to the Place of Gathering in the Next World to meet his Reckoning. There will

1. Muslim related that Jabir ibn 'Abdullah stated, "I heard the Prophet, may Allah bless him and grant him peace, said, 'Every slave will be raised according to how he died.'" 'Abdullah ibn 'Umar stated that he heard the Messenger of Allah, may Allah bless him and grant him peace, say, "When Allah desires to punish a people, He punishes those who are among them and then they will be resurrected according to their intentions." (al-Bukhari)

also be the two guardian angels who recorded all his actions during his life in this world. Every person will be gathered together with his partner from the jinn.

The sun will draw near to the people.[1] It may not be the same as the sun of this world but the important thing is that it will give off a heat many times greater than in this world. Creatures will be barefoot and naked.[2] Their feet will be useless to them owing to the crush of the crowd. All creatures will surge against one another, jostling each other because of the intensity of their torment and anxiety. The sun's blaze will mingle with the hot steam of people's breath and with the heat of the eruptions from the earth. Burdens will be heavy; hearts will burn; and fear and shame will envelop them at the prospect of being presented to Allah. Sweat and tears will flow and stream onto the earth, mixing with its soil.

The level of sweat will rise against people's bodies according to the quantity of their sins. But this will not affect all bodies - not those of the Prophets and the people of knowledge who learnt and taught knowledge, nor those of the truthful and the martyrs. All of these and some others as well will be sheltered on that critical Day by the shade of the Throne of the All-Merciful. The heat of the sun will not touch them and no sweat will come from them. Joy will spread over their faces. They will converse with the angels with love and welcome. My God! O the immensity of Your power and the vastness of Your mercy! As Your noble Messenger informed us: "Allah has a hundred mercies. Among them is one mercy which creatures show to one another, and ninety-nine are for the Day of Rising." (Muslim)

1. Ibn Hanbal relates from al-Miqdad ibn al-Aswad al-Kindi that he heard the Messenger of Allah, may Allah bless him and grant him peace say, "On the Day of Rising, the sun will draw near to people until it is about a mile or two miles away from them." He said, "The sun will sap them and they will find themselves sweating according to the actions they did. It will reach the ankles of some, the knees of others, the waists of others, and some will have their mouths submerged by it." (Muslim has it from Yahya ibn Hamza, and at-Tirmidhi from Ibn Jabir.)

2. A'isha reported that she heard the Messenger of Allah, may Allah bless him and grant him peace, say, "People will be gathered barefoot, naked and uncircumcised on the Day of Rising." She asked, "Messenger of Allah, men and women together looking at one another?" He replied, "'A'isha, the event will be too grave a matter for them to look at one another." (Agreed upon)]

There is one man to whom Allah gave the blessing of power and rank and who ruled in this world. He upheld the laws of his Lord and was just in his rule. He was a humble, just, believing ruler and at the same time a noble, charitable person whose left hand did not know what his right gave away.

There is another who was deprived of rank and power. Poverty and abasement were his lot. But he was patient and anticipated his reward from Allah. Whenever an opportunity came to him to enjoy any of the things of this world which he did not possess, he refused anything which Allah had not made lawful.

There are also people who loved one another for the sake of Allah.[1] They did not love one another or befriend one another for the sake of any worldly advantage. They were attracted to one another by their love for Allah alone. Friendship gathered them together with all the truthfulness, fidelity, sacrifice and self-denial which that entails, so that each of them wanted for his brother what he wanted for himself. They met together for the sake of remembering Allah. They helped one another to righteous action based on desiring only what would please Allah.

There are others who busied themselves with helping people in distress.[2] No one sought their assistance in a time of need without their striving to the utmost to save them from whatever affliction they were facing without any expectation of thanks or repayment. They did it purely out of a desire for the Face of Allah.

Another person grew up immersed in the worship of Allah, his heart being attached to the mosque. Whenever he remembered Allah when he was alone his eyes overflowed with tears out of humility and love of Allah.

---

1. Muslim transmitted in his *Sahih* in the Chapter of Virtues from Abu Huryara that the Messenger of Allah said, may Allah bless him and grant him peace: "Allah will say on the Day of Rising: "Where are those who loved one another for the sake of My majesty? Today I will shade them on a day in which there is no shade but My shade."

2. Ka'b ibn 'Amr stated that the Messenger of Allah said, may Allah bless him and grant him peace, "If anyone grants a respite to someone in difficulties or reduces what he owes, Allah will shade him in His shade." (Muslim) Muslim reported that Abu Hurayra related that the Messenger of Allah, may Allah bless him and grant him peace, said, "Whoever relieves a Muslim of one of the cares of this world, Allah will relieve him of one of the cares of the Day of Rising.

All these people[1] and all men and women like them will find that their actions were not performed in vain.

On that fearful day they will enjoy the shade of the Throne of the All-Merciful while the remainder of Allah's servants who are gathered with them in the same place will have the sun blazing down on them and sweat will pour from them, as we have already heard, according to the amount of their sins until some become almost completely submerged in it! Shaytans, serpents, scorpions, tigers, vultures, and other terrors will encircle the unbelievers according to their sins and errors. An indescribably foul smell will exude from their sweat and they will feel terrible oppression and hardship. Their movements will be cumbersome. They will try to stand straight but the throngs around them will push them over and the angels behind them will drive them on. They will be alarmed and terrified. They will want to shout or cry out but will not be able to. They will not be able to breathe. They will be forced to swallow foul water. They will be drowning. They will be choking. Death will come at them from every side. They will want it and try to meet it but it will swiftly be revealed that it is just a mirage.

Seeking intercession

Ages will pass and people will lose all track of time, not knowing how long has passed since the moment of Resurrection. The succession of day and night will have ended. The way that time is measured will be different and people's experience of time will be short or long according to their actions.

1. It is affirmed in the *Sahih* in a *hadith* from Abu Hurayra that that the Messenger of Allah, may Allah bless him and grant him peace, declared: "There are seven whom Allah will shade with His shade on the day when there is no shade but His shade (one variant has "the shade of His Throne"): a just Imam; a youth who grows up worshipping Allah; a man whose heart is attached to the mosque from when he leaves it until he returns to it; a man who refuses the advances of a noble and beautiful woman, saying, 'I fear Allah'; two men who love each other for the sake of Allah, meeting and parting for that reason alone; a man who gives *sadaqa* and conceals it so that his left hand does not know what his right hand gives; and a man who remembers Allah when he is alone and whose eyes overflow with tears."

"...A day with your Lord is the same as a thousand years in the way you count." (22:47)

"He directs the affair from heaven down to earth. Then it rises back up to Him in a day whose length is a thousand years in the way you count." (32:5)

"The angels and the Spirit ascend to Him in a day whose duration is fifty thousand years." (70:4)

The sole reality that will concern people during all this time will be the fact that the sun is still burning their bodies and their hearts. They will not know how long it has been going on. The unbelievers will be immersed in a sea of sweat, sweat which will completely cover their heads and scald their bodies by the intensity of its heat. The only thing they will be able to do is struggle with their hands above their heads, trying in vain to save themselves from drowning. But although they drown they will not die. They will lose the power to think or speak or even to ask for help. If someone were exposed indefinitely to the blazing heat of the sun in this world they would eventually die and escape from its torment. If they experience the anguish of drowning it only lasts a few moments and they are quickly dead. But in the Next World they will be exposed to all this and more for endless periods and they will never die.

Some believers, as we have seen, will have shade beneath the Throne of the All-Merciful but others will experience the blaze of the sun according to the extent of their sins, alleviated by the degree of their belief. Those believers will be dismayed and will call out:[1] "Our Lord, save us from this punishment! Give us relief from this affliction, even in the Fire! Is there no one to intercede for us with You? Where is our progenitor Adam? Is he not saddened by the evil state of his descendants? Will he not strive to relieve us of our distress?"

"O Adam! You are the father of mankind! Allah chose you[2] and created you with His own hand. He breathed His spirit into you.

---

1. There are many traditions about intercession in the collections of *Hadith*.
2. *"Allah chose Adam and Nuh and the family of Ibrahim and the family of*

48

Did He not make the angels prostrate to you? Did He let you dwell in the Garden and teach you the names of all things? Do you not see the situation we are in? We hope that you will intercede for us with your Lord."

Adam will wish that he could do something for them and will say to them, "You had your opportunity in the world. The All-Aware gave you a reprieve while you were there. Perhaps you now want to return to it and repent but you cannot do that. Here you are today after wasting every opportunity of salvation you were given, seeking my intercession to rescue you from the punishment and gain admittance to the Garden. Why come to me when I was the reason for mankind's expulsion from Paradise? I disobeyed my Lord and ate from the tree He forbade me to eat from. Now I fear for myself on account of my error on this Day when my Lord is unprecedentedly angry. Go to someone else. Go to Nuh. He is the Messenger whom Allah sent after me to the people of the earth."

Glory be to Allah! How can Adam think his error punishable? The descent of man to the earth was decreed and written and unavoidable. Allah wished to prepare the human creature acting as His Viceregent in the earth and to make him aware of the existence of His will and call his attention to the conflict which awaited him between his animal desires, which Shaytan makes seem so attractive, and his covenant with His Creator. It was the first test of the human being. How could Adam fear an error for which he has repented and been forgiven? Allah says in His Mighty Book:

"Adam disobeyed his Lord and became misled. But then his Lord selected him and turned to him and guided him."
(20:121-122)

Mankind will call out: "O Nuh! You are our father after Adam! You were one of the first Messengers to the people of the earth and Allah called you a 'grateful slave.'[1] Do you not see the state we are in? Please intercede for us with your Lord!"

'Imran over all other beings - descendants one of the other. Allah is All-Hearing, All-Knowing." (3:33-34) The family of 'Imran means 'Isa and his mother Maryam.

1. *"O descendants of those whom We carried with Nuh! He was a grateful slave." (17:3)*

Nuh will reply, "I am not a fit intercessor. I asked my Lord for something without knowledge. Today He is wrathful with an anger beyond compare. Go to Ibrahim. He is the Friend of Allah."

Can a man be so ashamed of a single small slip he committed in a life characterised by struggle in the Cause of Allah for 950 years?

> *"We sent Nuh to his people and he remained among them a thousand years less fifty. The Flood seized them and they were wrongdoers."* (29:14)

After the Flood and the death of his son, Nuh felt the grief of a loving father and he remembered his Lord's promise to save his family:

> *"Nuh called out to his Lord and said, 'My Lord, my son is one of my family and Your promise is surely the Truth; and You are the justest of judges.'"* (11:45)

A vehement response came from his Lord which resembles a rebuke:

> *"He said, 'Nuh, he is definitely not of your family. He is someone whose action is not righteous. Do not, therefore, ask Me for something about which you have no knowledge. I admonish you lest you should be one of the ignorant.'"* (11:46)

The truth which Nuh neglected was that 'family' in the sight of Allah are those near of creed and not those near of blood. That son who did not believe in the Message of his father, the believing Prophet, was therefore not considered one of his family. Nuh trembled when the reply came to him, fearing that he had erred in respect of his Lord. He sought refuge in Him and asked for His forgiveness and mercy.

> *"He said, 'My Lord, I seek refuge with You from asking You for anything about which I have no knowledge. If You*

50

*do not forgive me and have mercy on me, I will be among
the lost.'"* (11:47)

Allah's mercy was immediately given to Nuh and He forgave
and blessed not only him but all his righteous descendants.

> *"It was said, 'O Nuh! Descend with peace from Us and
> with blessings on you and the nations which issue from
> those who are with you. But there are nations to whom We
> shall give enjoyment and then a painful punishment from
> Us will afflict them.'"* (11:48)

> *"Nuh called out to Us, and what an excellent response
> We gave! We rescued him and his family from the terrible
> plight and made his descendants the survivors and left
> later people saying of him: 'Peace be upon Nuh among all
> beings!' That is how We recompense the good-doers. He
> was truly one of Our believing slaves. Then We drowned
> the rest of them."* (37:75-82)

Yet even after all this kindness from Allah, Nuh remembers the
slip he made and feels ashamed to meet his Lord with it on the
Day of Rising.

Then mankind will turn to Ibrahim, "O Ibrahim! You are the
Friend of the All-Merciful! You are the father of mankind and the
father of the Prophets. We intercede with you to intercede for us
with your Lord to save us from this dire adversity."

But Ibrahim will say, "How can I? I lied in this world, so how
can I face my Lord today? Go to someone else. Go to Musa, to
whom Allah spoke and gave the Torah."

The lies he is referring to are his words, "I am sick" and "No,
this one, the biggest of them, did it." After Ibrahim despaired of
his people reponding to his call to them to worship the One God,
he decided to smash the idols they worshipped. On one feast day
his people placed food in front of their idols as an offering and
prepared to go out to their recreation grounds outside the city.
They invited Ibrahim to go with them, but he refused saying, *"'I
am sick.'"* (37:89) He said that so that he would have the opportu-

51

nuity to carry out the righteous action he had resolved on, which had no evil in it. And the truth was that he actually was sick, filled with sorrow and care at the disbelief and obduracy of his people.

When he was left alone, he went swiftly to the idols and looked at the food in front of them and asked them ironically, *"'Do you not eat?'"* (37:91) Of course the idols did not reply. He wanted to give his people a practical demonstration of the futility of their superstitions after all his good advice to them had failed, so he destroyed all the idols except for one.

"Then he turned on them striking with his right hand." (37:93)

"He broke them into pieces, except the biggest one, so that they should have it to consult!" (21:58)

When the people returned they found all their idols smashed except the largest of them. They were very upset, being tradition-bound and blinded by superstition. They were completely unable to see that if the stones really had been gods they would surely have been able to defend themselves. They could think of nothing but avenging themselves on the idol-smasher, and the finger of suspicion pointed clearly at Ibrahim.

"They said, 'Did you do this to our gods, Ibrahim?'" (21:62)

They still said "our gods" and Ibrahim, peace be upon him, wanted to make them spontaneously admit that the idols were inanimate without perception or volition, not able to speak or act so he addressed them.

"He said, 'No, this one, the biggest of them, did it. Ask them – if they are able to speak!'" (21:63)

This was not in reality a lie because his people knew for certain that the idol which had been carved by human hand from stone could neither help nor harm anyone or anything. But despite that they worshipped it as a custom because they had found their fathers doing so. They worshipped it because their hearts and minds too had turned to stone! Ibrahim's intention in replying to them in the way that he did was to open the minds and hearts of those foolish people so that they might become free from blind custom. And in fact for a moment a chink opened but it swiftly closed up again.

> "They consulted among themselves and said, 'It is you yourselves who are wrongdoers.' But then they relapsed back into their unbelief: 'You know full well that these idols cannot speak.'" (21:64-65)

Thus Ibrahim's untrue statement was not the result of cowardice. Ibrahim was certainly no coward. He was strong and courageous, steadfast and forbearing, firm in belief, intellect and will. There was nothing that would ever induce him to lie. Ibrahim did not fear his people. When he said, *"You know full well that these idols cannot talk,"* he established proof against them. They acknowledged openly that their gods could not talk but despite that they continued to worship other than Allah. Ibrahim reacted and immediately addressed them with boldness and courage.

> "He said, 'Do you then worship, instead of Allah, what cannot benefit you or harm you in any way? Shame on you and what you worship besides Allah! Will you not use your understanding?'" (21:66-67)

Ibrahim desired good for them and they desired evil for him. All their proofs failed them and they were unable to find any response except resorting to force.

> "They said, 'Burn him and support your gods if you are resolved to do something.'" (21:68)

So Ibrahim, peace be upon him, did not lie when he said, *"I am sick,"* or when he said, *"No, this one, the biggest of them, did it."*

If they had been lies Allah Almighty would have been angry at him. But Ibrahim experienced only Allah's pleasure and mercy. When the people ordered him to be burned something else happened. All their tricks were thwarted and all their actions made futile. The Word of Allah is all that counts and His Command cannot be gainsaid.

> *"We said, 'O Fire, be coolness and peace for Ibrahim!'*
> *They desired to entrap him but We made them the losers."*
> (21:69-70)

Allah says of Ibrahim in His Book:

> *"Who could have a better* deen *than he who submits himself completely to Allah and is a good-doer, and follows the religion of Ibrahim, a man of pure natural belief. Allah took Ibrahim as a close friend."* (4:125)

Yet even despite this Ibrahim will feel that he is not competent to act as an intercessor for mankind on the Last Day.

Mankind will then resort to Musa: "O Musa! You to whom Allah spoke![1] We implore you to intercede for us with the Lord of the Worlds. He chose you for His Message and Word[2] over all the people of the entire world in your time. Does our distress not sadden you?"

Musa will say, "I am not fit to intercede. I killed a man whom I was not commanded to kill. Perhaps my Lord will show mercy to me on this critical day. You must turn to the Word of Allah and His Spirit, 'Isa."

> *"When he reached maturity and came of age, We gave him right judgement and knowledge. That is how We repay those who do good. He entered the city at a time when its people were unaware and found there two men fighting: one from his faction and the other from his enemy. The one*

---

1. *"And Allah spoke directly to Musa."* (4:164)
2. *"He said, 'Musa! I have chosen you over all mankind for My Message and My Speech. Take what I have given you and be one of the thankful.'"* (7:144)

from his faction asked for his help against the other from his enemy. So Musa hit him with his fist, dealing him a fatal blow." (28:14-15)

It was only a single blow from Musa and the man died. Musa was a strong man. He had swallowed the bitterness of Pharaoh's injustice and his persecution of his people of the Tribe of Israel. He saw one of Pharaoh's men attacking an Israelite who asked him for help. He reacted and became angry. He quickly went to his assistance, hit the Egyptian with a single blow and the man fell to the ground, dead. Musa was alarmed. Confusion and disquiet assailed him. He had not intended to kill the man. He had only wanted to rescue a wronged person from his oppressor. Musa was dismayed. What should he do now? How could he gain his Lord's forgiveness for his crime? Is that how easy it is to become a murderer? Many questions assailed his mind. He regretted what he had done in his anger. Anger provides an open door for Shaytan.

"He said, 'This is Shaytan's work. He is an open and clear misleading enemy.'" (28:15)

Musa's entire being was shaken and he turned to his Lord to acknowledge his wrong action and supplicated to him to seek His forgiveness.

"He said, 'O Lord, I have done myself wrong. Forgive me.' So He forgave him. He is the Forgiving, the Merciful." (28:16)

When his Lord forgave him he became aware of the immensity of His blessing upon him. He had given him wisdom, knowledge and strength. He had blessed him often before. Finally He gave him the blessing of forgiveness. Musa promised his Lord to never to support any evildoer.

"He said, 'O Lord, because of Your blessing to me, I will not be a supporter of evildoers.'" (28:17)

That is how Musa accidentally erred and then regretted it and turned to Allah, and His Lord forgave him and pardoned him. Thus Musa was innocent before his Lord of the crime of murder and being an evildoer. In spite of that, he will be too ashamed on the Day of Rising to face Him.

This incident which was the cause of Musa's flight from Egypt contains far-reaching wisdom. The events of Musa's life produced that great being who was not only a Prophet of the tribe of Israel but also, in a way, the progenitor of the world we live in today. Allah wanted to test Musa in order to train him and prepare him for his chosen role. One of his tests was his fear and flight from Pharaoh, forcing him to leave his family and homeland and go into exile with a simple way of life after having been affluent and comfortable in the palace of the greatest king on earth.

Musa passed through many tests over the course of many years and he proved steadfast and firm until he was mature and ready to bear the greatest responsibility at the predetermined time. The command of Allah came and Musa returned to Egypt as one of Allah's Prophets.

> "...You killed a man and We rescued you from trouble and tested you with many trials. You stayed some years among the people of Madyan. Then you arrived at the predestined time, Musa! I have chosen you for Myself." (20:40-41)

> "Mention Musa in the Book. He was truly sincere and was a Messenger and a Prophet." (19:51)

The sun will continue to burn and the sweat to stream down and the waiting to go on. Mankind will cry out: "Can no one to intercede for us with Allah! Where is 'Isa? 'Isa! You are the Spirit of Allah and His Word![1] You are the slave and Messenger of Allah! Are you happy with our state? Will you not save us from what afflicts us?"

---

1. *"The Messiah, 'Isa son of Maryam, was only the Messenger of Allah and His Word, which He cast into Maryam, and a Spirit from Him."* (4:171)

'Isa will say, "I was taken for a god and worshipped alongside Allah. My Lord is angry today with an anger such as He has never shown before and never will show again. If you truly want intercession, you must go to the Beloved of Allah and the Seal of the Prophets.[1] You must ask Muhammad. He is the One who has this station. Allah has forgiven his past and future wrong actions."[2]

Mankind will not find any intercessor with Allah except Muhammad, may Allah bless him and grant him peace. They will go to him and cry out with the tears pouring from their eyes and the sweat streaming from their bodies, saying, "Muhammad! O slave and Messenger of Allah! Do you not see the state we are in? Do you not see the distress which afflicts us? We cannot bear it. We beg you to intercede for us with your Lord. You are the Seal of the Prophets! You are the Beloved of Allah. He protected you from committing any wrong action. O Muhammad, do not disappoint us! Do not refuse to be our intercessor with the Lord of the worlds!" Muhammad, may Allah bless him and grant him peace, will agree to intercede for them with Allah.

Muhammad, may Allah bless him and grant him peace, will become the intercessor for mankind on the Day of Rising because Allah promised him the Praiseworthy Station[3] when He said:

1. *"Muhammad is not the father of any of your men, but he is the Messenger of Allah and the Seal of the Prophets. Allah has knowledge of all things."* (33:40)

2. *"We have indeed granted you a manifest victory, for Allah to forgive you your earlier wrong actions and any later ones and complete His blessing upon you, and guide you on a straight path; and for Allah to help you with a mighty help."* (48:1-3) This means that Allah decreed that he would be protected from lapsing into wrong actions.

3. Al-Bukhari transmitted from Jabir ibn 'Abdullah that the Messenger of Allah, may Allah bless him and grant him peace, said. "Whoever says. after hearing the *adhan*, 'O Allah, Lord of this perfect call and established prayer, give Muhammad the *wasila* (mediation) and superiority and raise him up to the Praiseworthy Station which You promised him, my intercession will be available for him on the Day of Rising."

According to the *Sahih* of Muslim, 'Abdullah ibn 'Amr ibn al-'As reported that he heard the Prophet, may Allah bless him and grant him peace, say, "When you hear the *mu'adhdhin*, repeat what he says and then ask for blessing on me. Whoever asks for blessing on me once, Allah blesses him ten times for it. Then he should ask Allah for the *wasila* for me. It is a station in the Garden which only one of Allah's slaves will have and I hope that I will be that one. Whoever asks Allah for the *wasila* for me, intercession will be available for him.

57

"And stay awake for prayer during part of the night as a supererogatory action for yourself. It may be that your Lord will raise you to a Praiseworthy Station."

(17:79)

This does not mean that intercession is confined to Muhammad, peace and blessings be upon him. All the Prophets, peace and blessings be upon them, are granted intercession. It is just that Muhammad, may Allah bless him and grant him peace, is singled out to initiate the process of intercession. He is the first to intercede and then there are other intercessions after that by Allah's permission. He said to people in this world, "Every Prophet has a supplication answered, and I wish to keep my supplication as intercession for my people in the Next World." (Al-Bukhari, from Abu Hurayra)

As we have seen, every Prophet will refuse to intercede, and will refuse with complete courtesy, and will direct mankind to the Last Prophet, who alone has the power to inaugurate intercession. All Prophets are protected from sins but at the same time they are human beings. The errors which each of them mentioned were only considered sins in respect of their station as Prophets; for them to have done so is the peak of noble Prophetic humility. The more knowledge someone has of his Lord and the closer he is to Him, the more love and humility and greater fear and awe of Him he will have. So the awe of the Prophets in that position will be a fear that is much more intense than the fear felt by the rest of mankind.

The Land of the Return

Mankind will be driven to a land as white as snow, on which no blood has ever been spilled or sin committed and where Allah has never been disobeyed. It is a place without mountains or hills and where there are no seas or ravines. It is a flat land with no elevation or depression of any kind, completely bare with no covering or barrier anywhere. There is no place on it to flee or hide.[1]

1. It is affirmed in the two *Sahih* collections from Sahl ibn Sa'd that the Prophet said, may Allah bless him and grant him peace: "People will be gathered

"On the day the earth is changed to other than the earth, and the heavens likewise, and they parade before Allah, the One, the Conquering." (14:48)

Terror will fill people's hearts. They have left the world of causality and have arrived in the Next World. In an instant they are in a new situation with a terrifying and disconcerting appearance having no connection with the means of this world with which they were familiar. They will move but they will stagger with the befuddlement of people who are confused and overpowered. They will reel to the right and left as if they were drunk.

"You will think people drunk although they are not drunk: it is just that the punishment of Allah is so severe." (22:3)

Family ties will be abandoned. A man will not bother to listen to the cry of his child or to help his brother. His heart will not be softened by the groan of his mother or his spirit stir at the sight of his father. No yearning to meet his wife after that long separation will move him. He will not be concerned with anything but flight. But there will be nowhere to flee to. The terror that he is experiencing will absorb him completely. Confused questions will occur to his mind. "How can I save myself from this dreadful terror? When will the Day of Rising end? Will there ever be an end to this terrible Day?"

"The Day a man will flee from his brother and his mother and his father, and his wife and his children – every

---

on the Day of Rising on a reddish-white earth like a loaf of pure white flour on which there are no landmarks of any kind."

The newly created earth will be called *as-Sahira* in the period between the Blast of Swooning and the Blast of Resurrection. Then people will be driven to it after the Blast of the Resurrection. But Allah knows best.

According to the *tafsir* of Ibn Kathir, pt. 2, p. 544, Abu Ja'far ar-Razi reported from ar-Rabi' ibn Anas from Ka'b about His words, *"On the day the earth is changed to other than the earth, and the heavens likewise,"* that the heavens will become gardens and the place of the sea will become a fire and the earth will be changed to other than the earth. But Allah knows best."

man among them will on that Day be fully occupied with his own concerns." (80:34-37)

At-Tirmidhi transmitted from Abu Hurayra, may Allah be pleased with him, that the Messenger of Allah said, may Allah bless him and grant him peace: "People will be gathered on the Day of Rising in three positions: on their knees, on their feet, and on their faces." A man said, "Messenger of Allah, how can they walk on their faces?" He replied, "He Who made them walk on their feet can make them walk on their faces." We read in the two *Sahih* collections, in a *hadith* related by Anas, that a man asked, "Prophet of Allah, will the unbelievers be gathered on their faces?" He said, "Is not He Who made people walk on their feet in this world able to make them walk on their faces in the Next World?"

So the unbelievers will go on their faces and bellies in the land of the Gathering on the Day of Rising.[1] In the midst of the crowd the feet of various creatures will tread on them. The pain and shrieking will be overwhelming. There will be no way for them to save themselves or even to die.

"Those who are herded headlong into Jahannam, such people are in the worst position. They are most misguided from the way." (25:34)

The conversation between the hypocrites and the believers

The place will be totally pitch-dark. That fearsome crowd of creatures of Allah will surge into one another. They will be forced together by the intensity of the darkness and the press of the throng. It is utter terror – terror of the Almighty. But the believers will have light which spreads out in front of them and on their right, lighting the way of each of them according to the good actions that they performed in this world. It will protect them

---

1. *"Is he better guided who goes grovelling on his face or he who walks upright on a straight path?"* (67:22)

against the evil of the darkness and the fright and the press of the crowd and will guide them to a safe path. It is a tremendous mercy from Allah Almighty which will surround His righteous servants on every stage of that interminable Day.

> *"The Day you see the believing men and women, their light streaming out in front of them and on their right. Good news for you today of Gardens with rivers flowing under them, to be in them timelessly forever. That is the Great Victory."* (57:12)

The hypocrites will hear that good news and will see the light of the believers, but their way will not be lit by it. They will try to catch up with them to borrow some of their light.

> *"The Day the men and women of the hypocrites will say to those who believe, 'Wait for us so that we may borrow a little of your light.'"* (57:13)

Then a powerful unidentified voice will say: "Go back behind you. Go back to the first world, to your actions. Light can only be obtained there." The hypocrites will be distressed. They will repeat in consternation, "Go back behind us? To our actions? How? Why? So that we can seek light?"

> *"It will be said, 'Go back behind and look for light!'"*
> (57:13)

The hypocrites will attempt to go back to look for light but they will be confused in the darkness. Their attempts will prove fruitless. Their feet will become entangled and they will bump into each other. In the deep darkness their true situation will become clear to them: "Our actions in the world were dark and black, so how can we expect to get any light from them today? We lived our life in the world in the darkness of hypocrisy and sowing dissension between people. We showed our brothers a counterfeit light of belief and false love while we concealed inside ourselves a pitch-black darkness of rancour, deception, intrigue and hypocrisy.

61

Today we are harvesting the fruits of our actions as darkness and torment, regret and misguidance." The hypocrites will be confounded and the believers guided.

"And a wall shall be raised between them with a gate in it, inside which there will be mercy but before whose exterior lies the punishment." (57:13)

Mercy will encompass the believers, while punishment encompasses the hypocrites. The hearts of the hypocrites will burn with a fire of intense exasperation and discontent. They are filled with malice towards the believers: "Were we not with you in the world? Did we not live together on the same earth? Were we not resurrected together on the same plain? Why are we now parted? Did we not pray and fast with you? Did we not peform the *hajj* and fight together?"

The believers will immediately reply, *"'Indeed you were ...'* All that you said was true. *'And yet you caused trouble for yourselves...'* You became dependent on the pleasures and transient appetites of the lower world. Not only that, but you lay in wait for the righteous slaves of Allah, hoping that evil would befall them, and you were in doubt about the Resurrection after death. You doubted the Day of Resurrection. You thought that you would not meet Allah and that the Almighty would not call you to reckoning or punish you. That is not all: *'false hopes deluded you'*. You listened to the whisperings of the shaytans of men and jinn. Their falsehoods deceived you. You believed their false promises. You were proud *'until Allah's command arrived. The Deluder deluded you about Allah.'* (57:14) Your life in the lower world came to an end and today you have been resurrected anew. Now you are completely certain that the promise of Allah is true and that the delusions of Shaytan are false. Now you try to flee from the punishment but that is impossible. Nothing will help you today. No creature will save you from the punishment of the Creator.

"You indeed were with us as you claim – but only with your bodies. Your souls were in confusion and constant doubt. You hated us and you dissembled and made it appear that you loved us.

You were showing off to people when you prayed and fasted and performed the rest of your actions which outwardly appeared righteous. In reality, things were the opposite of that. The truth is that you did not remember Allah in your hearts for a single day."

"Today no ransom will be accepted from you, or from those who rejected. Your refuge is the Fire. It is your master. What an evil journey's end!" (57:15)

The arraying and clothing of Allah's slaves

The Decisive Hour will now approach: the Hour of the Reckoning. The terrible tumult will end and everyone will be positioned, each in their place according to the degree of their belief. They will be arrayed in rows[1] to await presentation before Allah.

Garments will be brought for all mankind. First, the Prophets will be clothed in the most sumptuous garments,[2] then those below them according to the degrees of their belief. As for the evil-doing unbelievers, they will be clothed in garments of black pitch, designed to burn their bodies.

"You will see the evil-doers that day yoked together in chains, wearing shirts of tar, their faces enveloped in the Fire..." (14:49-50)

---

1. *"...You will see the earth laid bare and We shall gather them together, not leaving out a single one of them.They will be paraded before your Lord in ranks..."* (18:47-48)

2. Al-Bayhaqi transmitted in the Book of Names and Attributes from Ibn 'Abbas that the Messenger of Allah, may Allah bless him and grant him peace, said: "You will be gathered naked and barefoot, and the first to be clothed from the Garden will be Ibrahim, peace be upon him. He will be clothed in a robe from the Garden, and a throne will be brought and set to the right of the Throne. I will be brought and clothed in a robe of the Garden. Then a throne will be brought and placed for me at the leg of the Throne." The garments of the Garden will protect the believers from the hardships of the Gathering and the terrors of the Day of Rising.

The Coming of Allah and the Angels

"What are they awaiting but for Allah to come to them in the shadows of the clouds, together with the angels, in which case the affair will have been decided? All matters return to Allah." **(2:210)**

For the first and only time, all the human beings who existed from the beginning of creation until the Final Hour will be gathered together at one time in one place, standing naked on a vast new earth never before seen by any eye. There will no mountain or sea in it. There is no cover on it and no shelter of any kind. The decisive moment approaches. Light begins to pierce the murky darkness. Lights of various colours sparkle overhead. Beautiful voices reverberate in the distance.

All these voices and lights come from a great distance far above the huge gathering. Their source is angels and other heavenly creatures who were veiled from us in this world. In the Next World they will descend to the earth in various and extraordinary forms. The angels of the heaven of this world come down to earth in the Next and they outnumber all other creatures. They will range themselves around mankind, encircling them.

All the angels descend from the seven heavens in wave upon wave, descending[1] from one heaven after another, their wings scintillating with light in the midst of the darkness, their bodies trembling with awe and exaltation, their voices raised in glorification, praise and the proclamation that there is no god but Allah.[2]

---

1. *"The Day that Heaven is split apart in clouds, and the angels are sent down rank upon rank, the Kingdom that Day will belong in truth to the All-Merciful. It will be a hard Day for the rejectors."* (25:25-26

2. At-Tabarani reports that Jabir ibn 'Abdullah related that the Messenger of

The people of the earth will tremble at the terror of the Standing. The immensity of the bodies of the angels and their huge number of wings will terrify them.[1] Their blazing lights will dazzle them.[2] Some people will ask in bewilderment, "Is our Lord among you?"

The angels will be alarmed by that naive question. They will say with severity and anger, "Glory be to our Lord! He is not among us. He is coming." Mankind will be bewildered. They will turn about in dismay. Then the ceiling of the universe will descend above them. Terror! Where to run to? Is there any deliverance? Eyes will be lowered and bodies will tremble and hearts will be displaced and fly up from people's chests to their throats.[3] What is happening is that the Throne of Allah is drawing near to the earth, and upon it will be Allah Himself.[4] The Majestic will come to His slaves on His throne in the shadows of the clouds together with the angels. There will be an immense blinding light. Clumps of fine clouds will veil creation from seeing its Majestic Creator.

"...And that Day eight will bear above their heads the Throne of their Lord" (69:16-17)[5]

Allah, may Allah bless him and grant him peace, said, "There is no place in the seven heavens the size of a foot or span or palm but that there is an angel standing on it or an angel prostrating or an angel bowing. On the Day of Rising, they will all say, 'Glory be to You! We did not worship You as You deserved to be worshipped but we did not associate anything with You."

1. *"Praise belongs to Allah, the Bringer-into-being of the heavens and the earth, the Maker of the angels as messengers, possessing wings – two, three and four. He adds to creation in any way He wills. Allah is Powerful over all things ."* (35:1)

2. "Ibn Hanbal states that 'A'isha narrated that the Messenger of Allah said, may Allah bless him and grant him peace: "The angels were created from light, the jinn were created from smokeless fire, and Adam was created from what has been described to you."

3. *"And warn them of the Day of Immediacy when hearts rise, choking, to throats. The wrongdoers will have no good friend nor any intercessor at their bidding. He knows the treachery of the eyes and what the hearts conceal."* (40:18-19)

4. *"The All-Merciful, established firmly on the Throne."* (20:5)

5. *"And heaven will be split apart, for that Day it will be very frail. And the angels will be gathered round its edges. And on that Day eight shall bear above their heads the Throne of their Lord. That Day you will be exposed and no concealed act of yours will remain concealed."* (69:16-17)

65

"You will see the angels circling round the Throne, glorifying the praise of their Lord..." (39:75)[1]

The angels, the Bearers of the Throne and the Cherubim[2] will descend close above mankind. Their voices will resound powerfully in the hearing of the entire universe, shaking all existence: "Glory be to the Master of the Kingdom and the Domain! Glory be to the Lord of Might and Omnipotence! Glory be to the Living who does not die! Glory be to the One who causes death but does not die! The All-Perfect, All-Holy! The Lord of the Angels and the Spirit, All-Perfect, All-Pure. Glory be to our Lord Most High! Glory be to the Master of Power and Immensity! Glory be to Him! Glory be to Him forever and ever!"

On the Day of Reckoning Allah will be angry with His slaves who did evil with such anger as He has never displayed before. All human beings will tremble at it. The Bearers of the Throne and those around it brought near to Allah will glorify His praise and then ask forgiveness for His believing slaves and they will pray for them.

> *"Those who bear the Thone and all those around it glorify the praise of their Lord and believe in Him and ask forgiveness for those who believe: 'Our Lord, You encompass all things in mercy and knowledge! Forgive those who turn to You and who follow Your way, and safeguard them from the punishment of the Blazing Fire. Our Lord, admit them to the Gardens of Eden that You promised them and all of their parents and wives and offspring who are righteous. Truly You are the Almighty, the All-Wise. And safeguard them from evil acts. Anyone You safeguard that Day from evil acts, to him You have been truly merciful. And it is that that constitutes the Great Victory.'"*
>
> (40:8-9)

---

1. *"...All shall be settled between them with truth. And it shall be said, 'Praise belongs to Allah, the Lord of all the Worlds.'"* (39:75)

2. The Karubiyyun, the angels nearest to Allah who are considered the noblest of angels along with the Throne-bearers and are more numerous than all creation.

To those who rejected faith a proclamation will be made:

*"Allah's hatred is far greater than your hatred of your-
selves since you were summoned to belief but then disbe-
lievted."* (40:10)

*"And your Lord comes, and the angels rank upon
rank."* (89:22)

The Throne-bearers and Cherubim will come down to the earth
and Allah will command that His Footstool be placed[1] wherever
He wishes on His earth. His Throne will remain above mankind
like a ceiling over their heads, resplendent, terrible, and unimagin-
ably vast. Allah will settle Himself on it in a way appropriate to
Himself without definition or limit.

*"And the earth will radiate with the pure Light of its
Lord..."* (39:69)[2]

---

1. In his *tafsir* Shuja' reported that Ibn 'Abbas said, "The Prophet, may Allah
bless him and grant him peace, was asked about the words of Allah, the Mighty
and Majestic, *'His Footstool embraces the heavens and the earth.'* (2:255) He
said, 'His Footstool is the place of His feet and no one can calculate the extent of
the Throne except Allah Almighty."

We find in a *hadith* related by Abu Dawud that the Messenger of Allah said,
may Allah bless him and grant him peace: "The Might of Allah is more immense
than that His Throne is over His heavens like this," and he made the shape of a
dome with his hand.

According to another *hadith*: "The seven heavens and the earth and what is
between them and what is in them in relation to the Footstool are like a ring cast
into a desert. The Footstool and what it contains in relation to the Throne is like
that ring in that desert." [The Footstool is not the Throne. The Footstool is under
the Throne and is far smaller than it. The Throne is the ceiling of all creatures and
the greatest of them. The Throne contains immense expanses, height and resplendent beauty, but it is beyond the power of any human being to describe it or imagine its form. Knowledge of it is with Allah alone. The light of the Throne is from
the Light of the Noble Face of Allah. The Throne has bearers who will carry it
and Allah Almighty is settled on it, in a way that is beyond definition.

2. According to the *tafsir* of Ibn Kathir, pt. 4, p. 270, 'Ikrima said, "If Allah
had placed the sight of all human beings, jinn, animals and birds in the eyes of a
single creature and then removed one single veil of the seventy veils between it
and the sun, he would not be able to look at it. The light of the sun is only a sev-

Humankind will be astounded and will stand in bafflement. The darkness will have completely disappeared. A pure eternal light will be everywhere - intensely strong, an unparallelled light. This light will dazzle the eyes of the believers and blind the eyes of the unbelievers. People's eyes will overflow with tears which will pour down their cheeks and many different feelings will flood forth. The unbelievers will shudder with anxious dismay and sheer panic. They will be increased in abasement and contrition. Even believers will be in turmoil, their hearts flooded with humility and reverence.

> *"Hearts that day will be pounding and eyes will be downcast."* (79:8-9)

All existence will be shaken. It will tremble out of fear and apprehension. A violent earthquake will run through it. Existence will turn to face its Lord, trembling in fear. All voices will be stilled. The billions of angels – and the billions of jinn and human beings[1] – will all stand on that vast plain in humility and dreadful silence. Majesty will settle over the Standing. There will be no influence or power, no kingdom or strength, except with Allah, the One, the All-Conquering, the Pure King, the Compelling Protector.

An all-engulfing silence will prevail everywhere.

> *"Voices will be humbled to the All-Merciful and nothing but a whisper will be heard."* (20:108)

---

entieth part of the light of the Footstool, and the light of the Footstool is only a seventieth part of the light of the Throne, and the light of the Throne is only a seventieth part of the light of the Veil. So think of the strength that Allah gives to His servant's eyes at the moment of looking directly at the Noble Face of his Lord!"

1. *"...You will see the earth laid bare and We shall gather them together, not leaving out a single one of them. They will be paraded before your Lord in ranks: 'You have come to Us just as We created you at first. Yes indeed, athough you claimed that We would not fix an assignation for you."* (18:47-48)

The Timescale of the Next World

"The angels and the Spirit ascend to Him in a day
whose duration is fifty thousand years." (70:4)

Allah created measurable time and subjected it to His will. He is equally able to create another kind of day, whose duration is a thousand years:

> *"He directs the affair from heaven down to earth. Then*
> *it rises back up to Him in a day whose length is a thou-*
> *sand years by your reckoning."* (32:5)

There is no contradiction in the Signs of Allah. There is nothing of which the power of Allah is incapable, it being unbounded by any limit whatsoever. A 'day' is a measure of time, and a day in the Next World has a completely different gauge from one in this world. A day in this world is defined by the rising and setting of the sun. Even then it is relative, varying greatly in different locations or planets in some of which the sun shines for days or months, or sets and does not appear for days or months.

The universe is in constant movement: the sun moves through space and its planets move with it. Everything is also in a state of constant rotation: the earth rotates on its axis and revolves around the sun; the moon revolves more swiftly round the earth; the sun rotates on its axis; the galaxies too rotate continually.

> *"And the sun runs to its determined place. That is the*
> *ordaining of the Almighty, the All Knowing."* (36:38)

> *"He has subjected for you the sun and the moon, hold-*
> *ing steady to their courses, and He has subjected for you*
> *the night and the day."* (14:32)

This is how linear time is defined: night and daytime, days and weeks, months and years, centuries and millennia. Time differs from one planet to another acccording to the power of gravity and the speed of rotation. Indeed, it also varies from one galaxy to another. A day defined by the rising and setting of the sun may be twenty-four hours as is the case on our planet, earth. Yet even then Allah is able to make people's experience of passing time faster or slower as He pleases. Imam Ahmad ibn Hanbal related from Abu Hurayra that the Messenger of Allah, may Allah bless him and grant him peace, declared, "The Last Hour will not come until time becomes so short that a year will be like a month, a month like a week, a week like an hour and an hour like the burning of a palm leaf."

Whatever causes there might appear to be in this world for anything that happens, the true cause in every case is the Power of Allah. If He wishes He can make the day of this world behave according to the accepted norms, or if He wishes He can abrogate them completely. How much more will this be the case in the Next World when the Power of Allah is completely unveiled!

A day in the Next World will last as long as the event for which it is intended. Allah will make it obey His wishes. The Day of Rising is one of the days of the Next World to which only the criteria of the Next World apply, criteria which we cannot understand now and which can only be explained to us in terms similar to those we use in this world. It is not a day in the sense of being a night and a day. It is a day defined by the specific events which occur in it – one which only Allah knows. No one can define its duration except Allah.

It is the Day on which Allah settles the accounts of His slaves. The Almighty has no need whatsoever to pause for rest. He does not have to spread the Reckoning over a number of days. All the events will follow one another on a single day, a day which begins with the Last Hour and continues until all human beings have reached their places in the Garden or the Fire.

The duration of the Day of Resurrection will be like fifty thousand years according to the way we measure time in this world, but it will be experienced differently by different people. A righteous believer will find it very short and easy, easier than the prescribed prayers which he prays each day in this world. The same day will seem to last hundreds of years to a believer who has committed wrong actions; and a thousand years or so to an unbeliever whose acts of disobedience were relatively few; and more or less than that, in proportion to the actions a person has done.

In a *hadith* from Abu Sa'id al-Khudri, may Allah be pleased with him, we learn that the Messenger of Allah, may Allah bless him and grant him peace, said, "On a day whose duration is fifty thousand years." Abu Sa'id exclaimed, "How long that is!" The Prophet replied, may Allah bless him and grant him peace, "By the One Who has my soul in His hand, it will be easy for the believer, easier for him than the prescribed prayers you pray in this world."

Abu Hurayra said, "For the believer the Day of Rising will be like the time between *Dhuhr* and *'Asr*."

"They ask you to hasten the punishment. Allah will not break His promise. A day with your Lord is the same as a thousand years of your reckoning." (22:47)

The General Intercession and the Praiseworthy Station

"And how many angels there are in the heavens whose intercession is of no avail at all until Allah has given permission to those He wills and is pleased with them!" **(53:26)**

As we have seen, when the distress of Allah's slaves becomes intense, they will ask every Prophet in turn to intercede with his Lord until they reach Muhammad, may Allah bless him and grant him peace, and he will agree to intercede for them all with the Lord of the Worlds. Then Muhammad, may Allah bless him and grant him peace, will go to a place beneath the Throne and ask permission of his Lord and fall down in prostration. He will praise Him and glorify Him until the Almighty says to him, "Raise your head, Muhammad. Speak and you will be heard. Ask and you will be given. Intercede and your intercession will be granted."

> *"On that day intercession will bring no benefit except for him whom the All-Merciful has authorised and with whose speech He is well-pleased."* (20:109)

Muhammad, may Allah bless him and grant him peace, will ask for the Reckoning to be speeded up and for the final division between human beings to be made, that of all people from the time of Adam until the Last Hour – indeed, even from before the time of Adam, since creatures other than the children of Adam were created. Muhammad will intercede for them all to save them from the terror of that Standing – to give them respite from the torment

72

of waiting and the affliction of the Day of Reckoning so that their situation may be settled: whether in the Garden or in the Fire.

According to al-Bukhari, Ibn 'Umar, may Allah be pleased with him and his father, said, "On the Day of Rising people will fall on their knees, each community following its Prophet, saying, 'O so-and-so, intercede! O so-and-so, intercede!' until intercession reaches the Prophet, may Allah bless him and grant him peace. That is the Day when Allah will raise him to the Praiseworthy Station."

Truly Allah Almighty spoke the truth when He says in His Noble Book about His Final Messenger:

"We have sent you only as a mercy to all the worlds."
(21:107)

At-Tirmidhi related that Abu Hurayra, may Allah be pleased with him, reported that the Messenger of Allah, may Allah bless him and grant him peace, was asked about His words *"It may well be that your Lord will raise you to a Praiseworthy Station"* (17:179) and said, "It means intercession."

Other intercessions will also take place on the Day of Rising. The angels and Prophets will intercede. The marytrs and people of knowledge will intercede, as will the believers. Everyone will intercede in accordance with his actions. But Muhammad, peace and blessings be upon him, is unique in all existence in being granted the first intercession, in which he intercedes for all communities.

Let us reflect on the words of the Almighty:

"And stay awake for prayer during part of the night as a supererogatory action for yourself. It may well be that your Lord will raise you to a Praiseworthy Station."
(17:179)

Imam Ahmad related that the Prophet said, may Allah bless him and grant him peace: "When the Day of Resurrection comes I

73

shall be the Imam of the Prophets and their spokesman and the Possessor of the Staff, and this is no boast." (narrated by Ka'b)

In the *Sahih* of Muslim it is reported from Abu Hurayra that the Messenger of Allah said, may Allah bless him and grant him peace: "I am the Master of the children of Adam on the Day of Resurrection and the first over whom the grave will open; and I will be the first to intercede and the first whose intercession is accepted."

Imam Ahmad related from the *hadith* of 'Ali that the Messenger of Allah, may Allah bless him and grant him peace said, "I will occupy the Praiseworthy Station on the Day of Rising." A man of the Ansar asked, "What is that Praiseworthy Station?" He replied, "When you are brought naked, barefoot and uncircumcised, the first to be clothed will be Ibrahim. Allah will say, 'Clothe My friend.' Then two white seamless garments will be brought and he will be clad in them. Then he will sit facing the Throne. Then my garment will be brought and I will sit on His right in a Station which no one else has ever had, and the first and the last will envy me." He added, "There will be an opening from Kawthar to the Basin."

Imam Ahmad related from the Messenger of Allah, may Allah bless him and grant him peace, 'There is no Prophet who does not have a supplication which he makes in this world. I have stored up my supplication as intercession for my Community. I will be the master of the children of Adam on the Day of Resurrection and it is no boast. I am the first from whom the earth will split open and it is no boast. I will have the Banner of Praise in my hand and it is no boast. (The Prophets) from Adam onwards will be under my Ban-ner and it is no boast." (Narrated by Ibn 'Abbas)

Imams al-Bukhari, Muslim and others have made it clear that this general intercession for which Muhammad, peace and blessings be upon him, is singled out from the rest of the Prophets is what is meant by His words, "Every Prophet has a supplication which is answered, but every Prophet has already used up his supplication. I have stored up my supplication as intercession for my Community." People will seek that intercession by the inspiration of Allah Almighty until the Praiseworthy Station of its Prophet, which he has been promised on the terrible Day, is manifested.

After the intercession of Muhammad, peace and blessings be upon him, for all nations, his surpassing concern for his own Community and his love and compassion for them will be shown by his words: "O Lord, my Community! My Community!" It will be said, "O Muhammad, let those of your Community who have no reckoning to make enter the Garden." Then it will be said to each Prophet, "Let those of your community with no reckoning to make enter the Garden." After that the Reckoning will be carried out upon those of the Community of Muhammad who have to undergo it, and then upon the rest of the communities.

The Noble Qur'an has related the answered prayers of each of the noble Prophets of Allah, peace and blessings be upon them. We have heard about the prayer of the Prophet for his community. What were the prayers of the other Prophets?

The Prayer of Nuh

> *"Nuh said, 'My Lord, do not leave a single one of the rejectors on the earth! If You leave any they will lead Your slaves astray and spawn nothing but dissolute rejectors. My Lord, forgive me and my parents and all who enter my house as believers, and all believing men and believing women; and do not increase the wrongdoers except in ruin!"* (71:26-28)

Nuh, peace be upon him, was sent at the dawn of humanity. He encountered much opposition, obstinacy and arrogance but he was endowed with much fortitude and patience. He did not become restless or wearied. He was never overcome by despair in all of the 950 years he spent in a constant struggle to convey Allah's Message to the dissolute unbelievers of his time. But their very existence affected the believers because of the laws they instituted and the false misguiding customs they adhered to, which moulded the entire society. They were determined to block Allah's Message and prevent it from reaching anyone's heart, particularly those of the young who were being born and growing up in that corrupt environment.

The existence of those unbelievers became an insoluble problem – indeed a scourge which had to be eliminated, a raging epidemic for which there was no cure. There was no solution but eradication: a conclusive eradication of all corrupters. That was the only possible solution for humanity at the time. Therefore the supplication of Nuh was against his people rather for them. Allah's response was the Flood which completely obliterated their existence and washed the earth of the filth of their depravity, purified mankind of corruption, and saved them from utter ruin :

"We sent Nuh to his people and he remained among them a thousand years less fifty. The Flood seized them while they were wrongdoers. We rescued him and the Companions of the Ark and We made it a sign for every being." (29:14-15)

The Prayer of Ibrahim

"When Ibrahim said, 'My Lord, make this a land of safety and provide its people with fruits, those of them who believe in Allah and the Last Day.' Allah said, 'Whoever rejects, I will let him enjoy himself a little. Then I will drive him to the punishment of the Fire. What an evil journey's end!'"

"When Ibrahim raised the foundations of the House with Isma'il: 'Our Lord, accept this from us! You are the All-Hearing, the All-Knowing."

"Our Lord, make us both Muslims submitted to You, and our descendants a Muslim nation submitted to You. Show us our rites of worship and turn towards us. You are the Ever-Returning, the Most Merciful."

"Our Lord, raise up among them a Messenger from them to recite Your Signs to them and to teach them the Book and the Wisdom and to purify them. You are the Almighty, the All-Wise."

76

Those are some of the requests of Ibrahim and Isma'il, peace be upon them both, as recounted in *Surat al-Baqara* (2:126-129); and all of them were granted. The prayer of Ibrahim was granted, for Allah made Makka a land of safety and provided its people with abundant provision so that they could live in security and peace. Blood was not to be shed in it and fighting was not to mar it. They lived in comfort and abundance.

Al-Bukhari transmits from 'Abdullah ibn Zayd ibn 'Asim, may Allah be pleased with him, that the Prophet said, may Allah bless him and grant him peace: "Ibrahim made Makka inviolable and made supplication for it. I have made Madina inviolable as Ibrahim made Makka inviolable and I have made supplication for it in respect of its *mudd* and *sa'* [two measures of volume] just as Ibrahim made supplication for Makka."

Muslim reported from Abu Sa'id, may Allah be pleased with him, that the Prophet, may Allah bless him and grant him peace, said: "O Allah, Ibrahim made Makka inviolable and it remains. I make Madina inviolable between its two roads. So blood should not be shed there or weapons carried there for fighting nor trees felled there except for fodder. O Allah, bless us in our city! Allah, bless us in our *sa'*! O Allah, bless us in our *mudd*! O Allah, make it twice blessed!"

Allah Almighty answered the supplication of Ibrahim when Jibril came to him and taught him the *hajj* rites and his Community submitted to Allah and learned how to perform the duty of the *hajj*. The wheel of time moved on and generations followed one after another. The number of Muslims increased in various areas of the world and they still come to Makka every year from different parts of the world to perform the rites of *hajj*.

The prayer of Ibrahim, the father of the Prophets, was realised and coincided with the prior decree of Allah when after many centuries Allah sent a Messenger from the descendants of Ibrahim, from the descendants of of Isma'il, peace be upon both of them. He sent a Messenger from among the people of Makka, a Messenger from them to them, or rather to all human beings and jinn. He sent Muhammad, peace and blessings be upon him. Ibrahim was the first to mention Muhammad, peace and blessings be upon him and make him known to mankind. Generations passed waiting for the appearance of the Seal of the Prophets from the Arabs of Makka, from the descendants of Isma'il son of Ibrahim, until 'Isa son of Maryam, peace be upon him, openly articulated his name. He was the last of the Prophets of the tribe of Israel.

> *"When 'Isa son of Maryam, said, 'O Tribe of Israel! I am the Messenger of Allah to you, confirming the Torah which came before me and giving good news of a Messenger coming after me whose name is Ahmad.'"* (61:6)

When the Messenger of Allah, may Allah bless him and grant him peace, was asked, "Messenger of Allah, how did your mission first begin?" He replied, "The prayer of my father Ibrahim, and 'Isa's good news of me. And my mother dreamed that a light emerged from her which illuminated the castles of Syria." (Ahmad ibn Hanbal)

Allah Almighty says in *Surat al-A'raf* (7:154-159):

> *"He said, 'As for My punishment, I strike with it anyone I will. My mercy extends to all things, but I will prescribe it for those who are godfearing and pay the zakat, and those who believe in Our Signs: those who follow the Messenger, the Unlettered Prophet, the one they find written down with them in the Torah and the Gospel, commanding them to do right and forbidding them to do wrong, making good things lawful for them and bad things unlawful for them, releasing them from their heavy loads and the chains which bound them. Those who believe in him and honour him and help him, and follow the light that has been sent down with him, they are the successful.'*
>
> *"Say: 'O people of mankind! I am the Messenger of Allah to you all, from Him to whom the kingdom of the heavens and the earth belongs. There is no god but He. He gives life and causes to die. So believe in Allah and His Messenger, the Unlettered Prophet, who believes in Allah*

and His words, and follow him so that perhaps you will be guided.' Among the people of Musa there is a group who guide by the Truth and act justly in accordance with it."

There is another account of the prayer which was answered for Ibrahim, peace be upon him in *Surat Ibrahim*:

"Our Lord, I have settled some of my offspring by Your Sacred House in a valley with no cultivation, our Lord, that they may establish the prayer! Make the hearts of mankind incline towards them and provide them with fruits, so that perhaps they will be thankful." (14:37)

The Prayer of Musa

It was the attitude of the Tribe of Israel which led to the supplication which Musa made, peace be upon him, and which Allah Almighty answered. The account of these events comes in *Surat al-Ma'ida* :

"When Musa told his people, 'O my people! Remember Allah's blessing to you when He appointed Prophets among you and appointed kings over you, and gave you what He had not given to anyone else in all the worlds! O my people! Enter the Holy Land which Allah has ordained for you. Do not turn back in your tracks and so be transformed into losers.' They said, 'O Musa! There is a tyrannous people in it. We will not enter it until they leave it. If they leave it, then we will go in.'

"Two men among those who were afraid, but whom Allah had blessed, said, "Enter the gate against them! Once you have entered it, you will be victorious. Put your trust in Allah if you are believers.'

"They said, 'O Musa! We will never enter it so long as they are there. So you and your Lord go and fight. We will stay sitting here.'

"He said, 'My Lord, I have no control over anyone but myself and my brother, so make a clear distinction between us and this wantonly deviant people.' Allah said, 'The land shall be forbidden to them for forty years during which they will wander aimlessly about the earth. Do not waste grief on wantonly deviant people.'" (5:20-25)

Musa also made a supplication against Pharaoh and his nobles, which we hear about in *Surat Yunus*:

"Musa said, 'Our Lord, You have given Pharaoh and his nobles finery and wealth in the life of this world. Our Lord, may they be misguided from Your way. Our Lord, obliterate their wealth and harden their hearts so that they do not believe until they see the painful punishment.' He said, 'Your request is answered, so go straight and do not follow the way of those who do not know.' We brought the Tribe of Israel across the sea, and Pharaoh and his troops pursued them in their tyranny and enmity. Then, when he was on the point of drowning, he said, 'I believe that there is no god but Him in whom the tribe of Israel believe. I am one of those who submit as Muslims.'" (10:88-90)

Surat Taha recounts to us the supplication which Musa, peace be upon him, made to his Lord in the Holy Valley beside Mount Sinai when the Almighty placed on him the responsibility of conveying the message of *tawhid* to Pharaoh and his people. What a difficult task! Pharaoh was the richest and mightiest king on earth at that time, the one with the oldest civilisation, and the most unjust and tyrannical. Musa had lived in Pharaoh's palace and seen with his own eyes his injustice and tyranny. He had seen his armies and his nobles. He had killed one of them and fled – fled to Madyan out of fear that they would kill him. Despite all that, and after the passage of ten years, he returned to Egypt to confront that despotic tyrant. Musa was filled with unrestrained happiness at his Lord's pleasure with him in chosing him rather than any other creature to carry out that difficult task. But he wanted to be strengthened against Pharaoh and his council. That was his prayer. Allah Almighty answered him:

> "He said, "O Lord, expand my breast for me and make my task easy for me. Loosen the knot in my tongue so that they can understand my words. Assign me a helper from my family, my brother Harun. Strengthen my back through him and let him share in my task, so that we can glorify You much and remember You much, for You are watching us.' Allah said, 'Your request has been granted, Musa."
>
> (20:25-36)

The Prayer of 'Isa

Surat al-Ma'ida (5:111-115) recounts to us the story of the Table and the prayer of 'Isa, peace be upon him, and the response of Allah Almighty:

> "When I inspired the Disciples to believe in Me and in My Messenger, they said, 'We believe. Bear witness that we are Muslims who submit.' When the Disciples said, "Isa son of Maryam! Is your Lord able to send down to us a table out of heaven?' He said, 'Fear Allah if you are believers!' They said, 'We want to eat from it and for our hearts to be at rest and to know that you have told us the truth and to be among those who bear witness to it.' Isa son of Maryam said, 'O Allah, our Lord, send down to us a table from heaven to be a feast for us, for the first of us and the last of us, and a sign from You. Provide for us! You are the Best of Providers! Allah said, 'I will send it down to you. But if any of you subsequently rejects I will punish him with a punishment the like of which I will not inflict on anyone else in all the worlds!'"

The Prayer of Muhammad

All the Prophets of Allah, then, had prayers which were answered in this world. Why did Muhammad, peace and blessings be upon him, store up his as intercession for his community on the Day of Reckoning?

Imam Ahmad ibn Hanbal transmitted from 'Abdullah ibn 'Umar that the Prophet, may Allah bless him and grant him peace, said, "I was given a choice between being granted intercession or having half of my community enter the Garden. I chose intercession because it is more encompassing and more extensive. Do you think that it will be on behalf of the godfearing? No, it is for those who err and commit wrong actions."

Allah Almighty says in *Surat ad-Duha*:

> *"And truly your Lord will give to you, and you will be satisfied."* (93:5)

These words are said to mean, "Your Lord will give to you in the Next World until you are satisfied for your community and with the honour Allah has granted you.

Muslim transmitted from 'Abdullah ibn 'Amr ibn al-'As that the Messenger of Allah, may Allah bless him and grant him peace, recited the words of Ibrahim, peace be upon him, *"O my Lord! They have misguided many of mankind. Whoever follows me is with me but whoever disobeys me, You are Ever-Forgiving, Most Merciful,"* (14:36) and the words of 'Isa, peace be upon him: *"If You punish them, they are Your slaves. If you forgive them, You are the Almighty, the All-Wise."* (5:118) Then he raised his hands said, "O Allah! My Community! My Community!' and wept. Allah Almighty said, "Jibril, go to Muhammad and ask him why he is weeping." Jibril went to him and then informed Him - and Allah knows best - and He said, "Jibril, go to Muhammad and tell him, 'We will make you satisfied about your Community and will not sadden you.'"

Imam Ahmad ibn Hanbal related that in the year of the Tabuk expedition the Messenger of Allah, may Allah bless him and grant him peace, got up in the night to pray and some of his Companions gathered behind him and stayed with him until he had finished praying. He went out to them and said, "This night I was given five things which no one before me was ever given. I have been sent to all people, whereas those before me were sent to their own people alone. I was helped against the enemy with terror and even if there is a month's journey between me and them it will be filled with terror. Spoils of war and using them was made lawful for me while those before me thought it dreadful to use them. I was given the earth as a mosque and place of purity. Wherever I am when the prayer comes I can purify myself and pray. Those before me thought that dreadful. They used to pray only in their synagogues and churches. The fifth thing is that I have been told, 'Ask.' Every Prophet asked but I have delayed my request until the Day of Resurrection and it will be for me and for whoever bears witness that there is no God but Allah." (Also in Muslim, from 'Abdullah ibn 'Amr ibn al-'As)

How to obtain intercession

Jabir ibn 'Abdullah mentioned that the Messenger of Allah, may Allah bless him and grant him peace, said, "If anyone says, after hearing the *adhan*, 'O Allah, Lord of this perfect call and established prayer, give Muhammad the *wasila* (mediation) and the supreme rank, and raise him up to the Praiseworthy Station which You promised him, my intercession will be available for him on the Day of Rising." (Al-Bukhari)

Imam Ahmad transmitted from 'Abdullah ibn 'Amr ibn al-'As that the Messenger of Allah said, may Allah bless him and grant him peace: "When you hear the *mu'adhdhin*, repeat what he says and then ask for blessings on me. If someone asks for blessings on me once, Allah blesses him ten times for it. Then he should ask Allah for the *wasila* for me. It is a station in the Garden which only one of the slaves of Allah will have and I hope that I shall be that one. Whoever asks Allah for the *wasila* for me, intercession will be available for him."

The Almighty says in *Surat al-Ahzab*:

"Allah and His angels call down blessings on the Prophet. O you who believe! Call down blessings on him and ask for complete peace for him." (33:56)

Allah Almighty blesses the Prophet, praising him in the presence of the near angels. The angels then call down blessings on him. Allah commands the people of the earth to call down blessings on him and ask for complete peace and safety for him. All praise is combined for him: the praise of the people of the celestial world and that of the people of the terrestial world. Allah Almighty calls down blessings on all His Prophets and Messengers and on His believing slaves:

"O you who believe, remember Allah repeatedly, and glorify Him both morning and evening. It is He Who calls down blessing on you, as do His angels, to bring you out of darkness into the light, and to the believers He is Most Merciful." (33:41-43)

The blessing of Allah Almighty is mercy, and that of the angels is supplication and asking forgiveness. What then is that of human beings and jinn for the Prophets? We find in al-Bukhari that Ka'b ibn 'Ujra said, "Someone asked, 'Messenger of Allah, we know how to ask for peace on you, but how should we bless you?' He replied, 'Say: "O Allah, bless Muhammad and the family of Muhammad as You blessed Ibrahim and the family of Ibrahim. You are Praiseworthy, Glorious. O Allah, grant blessing to Muhammad and the family of Muhammad as You granted blessing to Ibrahim and the family of Ibrahim, You are Praiseworthy, Glorious."'"

Peace comes in the *tashahhud* in the words: "Peace be upon you, O Prophet, and the mercy and blessings of Allah." All who perform the prayer must ask for blessings on the Prophet, peace and blessings be upon him, in the final *tashahhud*.

Abu Talha, may Allah be pleased with him, reported that the Messenger of Allah, may Allah bless him and grant him peace, came out one day with joy shining in his face. He stated, "Jibril, peace be upon him, came and told me, 'Allah Almighty says, "Are you not satisfied, O Muhammad, that none of your Community asks for blessing on you without My blessing him ten times for it, and that none of your community asks for peace for you but that I wish peace on him ten times?"'" (Related by at-Tabarani)

Imam Ahmad ibn Hanbal related from 'Amir ibn Rabi'a that the Prophet, may Allah bless him and grant him peace, said, "If anyone asks for blessing on me the angels continue to ask for blessing on him as long as he is doing it for me. So let him do so for much or a little of that."

Imam Ahmad ibn Hanbal reported that Anas said, "The Messenger of Allah, may Allah bless him and grant him peace, said, "If anyone asks for blessing on me once, Allah blesses him ten times and removes ten errors from his record."

'Abdullah ibn Mas'ud, may Allah be pleased with him, stated, "The Messenger of Allah said, may Allah bless him and grant him peace: 'The person closest to me on the Day of Rising will be the one who has asked blessings on me the most.'" (at-Tirmidhi)

'Abdu'r-Rahman ibn Samura, may Allah be pleased with him, said, "The Messenger of Allah, may Allah bless him and grant him peace, came out to us and said, 'I saw an amazing thing last night. I saw one of my Community creeping along the *Sirat* for a time, then crawling on his hands and knees, then clinging to it. Then his blessings on me came to him and took him by the hand and kept him upright on the *Sirat* until he had crossed it." (at-Tabarani)

It is recommended to pray for blessings and peace on him when you visit his grave, may Allah bless him and grant him peace.

Abu Hurayra reported that the Messenger of Allah said, may Allah bless him and grant him peace: "Not one of you will ask for peace on me without Allah returning my soul to me so that I may return his greeting." (Abu Dawud)

Imam Ahmad ibn Hanbal transmitted from Ibn Mas'ud that the Messenger of Allah said, may Allah bless him and grant him peace: "The angels go through the earth conveying to me the greetings of peace from my Community."

Imam Ahmad ibn Hanbal transmitted that Aws ibn Aws ath-Thaqafi reported, "The Messenger of Allah, may Allah bless him and grant him peace, said, 'The best of your days is Friday. Adam was created and died on it. The Blast will occur on it. The Swooning will occur on it. So pray abundantly for me on Fridays. Your prayer is presented to me.' The Companions asked, 'Messenger of Allah, how will our prayer be presented to you when you have decayed?' He replied, 'Allah has forbidden the earth to consume the bodies of the Prophets.'"

Once a woman went to al-Hasan al-Basri, may Allah be pleased with him. She had a daughter who had died while still young and she wanted to see her in a dream. She said, "I have come to you so that you may teach me what I must do in order to see her."

He told her what to do and sure enough she did see her daughter in a dream but she saw her wearing garments of pitch with fetters on her neck and shackles on her feet. She told al-Hasan that and he was sad. After a time al-Hasan himself saw her but this time she was in the Garden with a crown on her head.

"Hasan, do you recognise me?" she asked, "I am the daughter of the woman who came to you so that you could teach her how to see me in a dream."

"How do you come to be here?" he asked her.

"A man passed by the place where we were," she replied, "and said the prayer on the Prophet, may Allah bless him and grant him peace, once. There were 550 people in torment in that graveyard. A voice commanded, 'Remove the punishment from them by the blessing of this man's prayer!"

What an immense blessing! On account of the blessing one man called down on Muhammad, may Allah bless him and grant him peace, they were all forgiven! So what do you think happens to someone who prays for him for years during the course of his life. Will he not gain his intercession on the Day of Resurrection?

With regard to the effect of the prayer on the Prophet on the living it has come down to us from the early Muslims that a man saw an extremely ugly being in the desert and asked it who it was.

"I am your bad actions," came the reply.

"What will deliver me from you?" he asked.

"Asking blessings on the Prophet as he said, may Allah bless him and grant him peace: 'Asking blessings on me is a light on the

Sirat. If anyone does so eighty times on the Day of *Jumu'a*, Allah will forgive him his wrong actions for eighty years.'"

It is related that a man who neglected to ask for blessings on our master Muhammad saw the Prophet, may Allah bless him and grant him peace, in a dream but the Prophet did not look at him. The man asked,

"Messenger of Allah, are you angry with me?"

"No," he replied.

"Then why do you not look at me?"

"I do not recognise you."

"How can you not recognise me when I am one of your Community and the men of knowledge report that you recognise your Community more readily than a mother recognises her child?"

"They spoke the truth," replied the Prophet, may Allah bless him and grant him peace, "but you did not ask for blessings on me, and my recognition of my Community is in accordance with the number of times they ask for blessings on me."

Then the man repented and asked for blessings on the Prophet a hundred times. Then he saw him in another dream and he, may Allah bless him and grant him peace, told the man, "Now I recognise you and will intercede for you." The man became a lover of the Messenger of Allah.

The position of Muhammad, may Allah bless him and grant him peace, entitles him to intercession and the Praiseworthy Station. Allah Almighty made the Prophets bear witness to His Messengership. The *deen* acceptable to Allah is but one. All the Messengers brought it. Allah took a covenant from every Messenger that he would follow the Messenger who would come after him and help him until coming of the Seal of the Messengers, Muhammad, came, peace and blessings be upon him.

> *"When Allah made a covenant with the Prophets: 'Now that I have given you a share of the Book and Wisdom, when a Messenger comes to you confirming what you already have, you must believe in him and help him.' Allah said, 'Do you agree and undertake My charge on*

that condition?' "We agree," they replied. He said, 'Bear witness! I will be one of the witnesses along with you.' So whoever turns away after that, they are wantonly deviant." (3:81-82)

The Unveiling of the Garden
and Hell-fire

"The Garden will be brought near to the godfearing.
The Blazing Fire will be displayed to the misled."
(26:90-91)

The earth will shine with the light of its Lord. Voices will be humbled to the All-Merciful. The slaves will continue to await the Decisive Moment, the Moment of the Reckoning. A dreadful silence will prevail. There will only be surreptitious whispers, a fearful frightened whispering. Moments pass – moments of the Next World which are like years in this world. What will be the reality of what we see! We have heard and read a great deal. We have spent time in reflection and imagination but its reality is beyond any depiction or conception. It is approaching. Its reality, as the Prophet, may Allah bless him and grant him peace, told us, is something which no eye has seen or ear heard and which has never occured to the heart of man.

The Garden will be brought near to the godfearing slaves of Allah, lofty and magnificient, radiating with light and resplendence. It is not just beautiful but far, far more. It is beyond splendour and beauty, above any imagination, beyond understanding. People will stand still in astonishment. Their eyes will be riveted. Their wits will leave them. Their hearts will cling to the sweetest hope. Truly the Garden is the highest and most sublime thing in existence.

The Fire, on the other hand, will be quite the opposite.

89

"And that Day Hellfire is brought near. That Day man will remember. But how will the reminder be for him?"

(89:23)

The Messenger of Allah, may Allah bless him and grant him peace, said, "Hell-fire will be brought on that day with seventy thousand thongs, each throng pulled by seventy thousand angels." (Muslim, from 'Abdullah ibn Mas'ud)

How can the fire of this world be compared with the Fire of the Next World? Abu Hurayra reported that the Prophet, may Allah bless him and grant him peace, said, "This fire of yours is only a seventieth of the Fire of Jahannam. The sea has been poured over it twice. Had it not been for that, Allah would not have put any benefit for anyone in it." (Ahmad)

Abu Hurayra also reported that the Messenger of Allah stated, may Allah bless him and grant him peace: "The Fire was kindled for a thousand years until it was red. Then it was kindled for another thousand years until it was white. Then it was kindled for yet a further thousand years until it was black. So it is black like the blackest night." (at-Tirmidhi and Ibn Maja)

'Umar ibn al-Khattab said, "Jibril came to the Prophet, may Allah bless him and grant him peace, at a time when he did not normally come to him. He said, 'Jibril, why do I see you with a changed countenance?' He said, "I did not come to you until Allah commanded the opening of the Fire." The Messenger of Allah, may Allah bless him and grant him peace, said, "Jibril, describe the Fire for me and inform me about Jahannam." He said, "Allah commanded it to be kindled for a thousand years until it was white. Then it was kindled for another thousand years until it was red. Then it was kindled for yet a further thousand years until it was black. It is dark black and its sparks do not give off light nor do its flames die down." He said, "By the One Who sent you with the truth, if one ring of the chain which Allah describes in His Book (69:32) were to be placed on the mountains of this world, it would melt them." The Prophet, may Allah bless him and grant him peace, said, "Enough, Jibril, Do not break my heart." The Prophet, may Allah bless him and grant him peace, looked at him weeping. He asked, "Jibril, you are weeping when you have the position you have with Allah?"

He replied, "How could I not weep? I do not know. Perhaps I have a position other than this in Allah's knowledge. Iblis was with the angels. Harut and Marut were among the angels." The Prophet, may Allah bless him and grant him peace, began to weep together with Jibril until a voice said, "Muhammad! Jibril! Allah has made you both safe from its violence."

Jibril left and the Prophet, may Allah bless him and grant him peace, went out. He passed by some of the Companions who were talking and laughing. He said, "You are laughing while Hell is in front of you! If you knew what I know, you would laugh little and weep much and you would have gone out to the hills seeking refuge in Allah Almighty." Allah revealed to him, "O Muhammad, I have sent you as a bringer of good news."

The Messenger of Allah, may Allah bless him and grant him peace, said, "Give good news, direct yourselves to what is right, and follow a middle course." (From Ibn Mardawayh)

Allah says:

> "They said, 'Do not go out to fight in the heat.' Say: 'The fire of Jahannam is far hotter, if only they understood.' Let them laugh little and weep much, in repayment for what they earned." (9:81-82)

The Fire will come and its dreadful horror will be unveiled: fearsome, terrifying. It will shudder in a tumult. It will groan and seethe. It will exhale towards the evil unbelievers. It will boil with rage. Its sound will reverberate through the place. It will be more terrible and awful than can be imagined, conceived or understood! Eyes will be riveted on it. Wits will vanish. The hearts will quake. All Existence will shake. Tears will flood out, tears of regret and remorse. The unbelieving jinn and human beings will shriek, "Alas! Woe! Affliction!"

All creation will repeat, both believer and unbeliever, "Myself, myself," except for Muhammad, peace and blessings be upon him, who will say, "My Community, my Community." A terrible and mighty voice will call out.

"They will be asked, 'Where are those whom you used to worship besides Allah? Can they help you or even help themselves?'" (26:92-93)

Silence will prevail. No answer will be heard. No answer is expected. It is simply a rebuke. People will fall to the ground out of the terror of the Standing. They will fall to their knees.

"You will see every nation on its knees." (45:28)

The Reckoning of the Birds and Animals

*"There are no creatures crawling on the earth or fly-
ing creatures, flying with its wings, who are not
nations just like yourselves. We have not omitted
anything from the Book. Then they will be gathered
to their Lord." (6:38)*

There is no living creature which inhabited the earth from the
beginning of creation until the Final Hour which will not be
brought back to life on the Day of Rising and then gathered and
arrayed together with the others of its species and stand for the
Reckoning. In this respect they will be just like human beings and
jinn. Every creature will be part of a nation. Allah will not forget
anything, not even the ant, fly or gnat. He - glory be to Him and
may He be exalted - did not forget anything in this world, so how
could He forget them in the Next World?

*"There is no creature on the earth whose provision is
not with Allah alone. He knows where it lives and where it
dies! They are all in a Clear Book." (11:6)*

*"How many a creature does not carry its provision
with it. Allah provides both for it and for you. He is the
All-Hearing, the All-Knowing." (29:60)*

However, human beings have to face a different kind of reckoning from that of the birds and animals. Are mankind, who took on
Allah's Trust of their own free will, on a par with other creatures?

*"We offered the Trust to the heavens and the earth
and the mountains and they refused to take it on and were*

93

very wary of it. But man took it on. He is indeed wrongdoing and ignorant." (33:72)

Is Allah's regent on the earth the same as other creatures?

"When your Lord said to the angels, 'I am putting a
regent on the earth.' They said, 'Are You putting on it one
who will corrupt it and shed blood while we glorify Your
praise and proclaim Your purity?' He said, 'I know what
you do not know.'" (2:30)

And what about the jinn? Are they the same as the birds and
animals in respect of the Reckoning – the jinn who disobeyed their
Lord, were arrogant before, and refused to prostrate before man?
The Reckoning will embrace every creature but requital is for
human beings and jinn alone.

"He will say, 'Enter into the Fire together with the
nations of jinn and men who passed away before you.'"
(7:38)
"We created many of the jinn and mankind for
Jahannam. They have hearts they do not understand with,
and eyes they do not see with. They have ears they do not
hear with. Such people are like cattle. No, they are even
further astray! They are the unmindful." (7:179)

The jinn, like human beings, include both believers and unbelievers. Allah will not let the action of any who do good deeds go
to waste. The reward of the unbelievers will be Hellfire and the
believers will have no other reward than the Garden.

"Whoever believes in Allah and acts rightly, He will
admit him into Gardens with rivers flowing under them, to
be in them timelessly forever without end. Allah has been
good to him with regard to provision." (65:11)

Messengers were not sent to human beings only: they were sent to both men and jinn. That is why punishment or reward will be meted out to both of them.

> "On the Day We gather them all together: 'O company of jinn! You gained many followers among mankind.' And their friends among mankind will say, 'Our Lord, we took benefit from each other, and now we have reached the term which You determined for us.' He will say, 'The Fire is your home. You will be in it timelessly, forever, except as Allah wills. Your Lord is All-Wise, All-Knowing.' Thus We make the wrongdoers friends of one another on account of what they have done. 'O company of jinn and men! Did not Messengers come to you from among you relating My Signs to you and warning you of the encounter of this Day of yours?' They will say, 'We testify against ourselves.' The life of this world deluded them and they will testify against themselves that they were rejectors."

(6:128-130)

Allah the All-Strong, the All-Conquering, Who created existence by the single word: 'Be!', Allah the All-Powerful who can obliterate any being in an instant, has threatened these two weak forms of creation and will attend to their reckoning after a period of deferral. It is a matter beyond any conception or depiction. It is an intense shaking terror.

Animals are sentient

Animals and all other creatures have their own spheres of existence, their own ways of life. They become friends and quarrel, rejoice and are pained. They see, hear and are aware, but in relation to their own worlds which the All-Seeing Creator brought into existence. This is confirmed by the incident of the Messenger of Allah, may Allah bless him and grant him peace, with the camel which had been shut up in a garden of the Banu'n-Najjar. No one could catch it or reach it until the Prophet came, may Allah bless him and grant him peace. When the camel saw him, it knelt before him. He said, may Allah bless him and grant him peace, "Bring the halter." When he had put the halter on it and saw that people were amazed at this, he turned to them and said, "There is nothing between the heavens and the earth which does not know that I am the Messenger of Allah, except for the rebels among men and jinn."

Besides this, it is reported from Abu Hurayra that the Messenger of Allah, may Allah bless him and grant him peace, said, "The best of days on which the sun rises is Friday. On it Adam was created, and on it he fell from the Garden. On it he was forgiven and on it he died. On it the Last Hour will occur, and every moving thing listens from morning until sunset in fearful anticipation of the Hour except men and jinn. During Friday there is a time when Allah gives to a believing slave standing in prayer whatever he asks for." (*al-Muwatta'*)

Animals have language

Animals and birds and every other creature have languages by which they communicate with one another. It is not the animals' fault that man does not understand them. Allah taught Sulayman, peace be upon him, the language of the birds and animals. He spoke and communicated with them.

> "*He inspected the birds and said, 'Why is it that I do not see the hoopoe? Or is he an absentee? I shall certainly punish him most severely or slaughter him or he must bring me clear authority.' But it did not delay for long and then it said, 'I have encompassed something that you have not, and I bring to you from Sheba definite news.'*"

(27:20-22)

Sulayman was able to understand and communicate with the

96

bird kingdom, and the same applied to the insect kingdom when he spoke with the ants.

"The troops of Sulayman were mustered for him, made up of jinn and men and birds, marshalled and formed into ranks. Then, when they reached the Valley of the Ants, an ant said, 'O ants! Go down into your homes so that Sulayman and his troops do not crush you without being aware of it.' He smiled, laughing at its words." (27:17-19)

Matter and plants are sentient

Even inanimate things and plants have sensation and feeling. They glorify and prostrate, like and dislike, weep and laugh. We do not see or hear this. We do not perceive it because we only live in our own world. But we read in the Noble Qur'an:

"There is nothing that does not glorify His praise, but you do not understand their glorification..." (17:44)

"Do you not see that everyone in the heavens and everyone on the earth prostrates to Allah, and the sun and moon and stars and the mountains, trees and beasts – and many of mankind?" (22:18)

The Prophet, may Allah bless him and grant him peace, said, "Allah forms the clouds and they speak with the best speech and laugh with the best laughter." (Ahmad ibn Hanbal, from an elder of Banu'l-Ghifar)

Heaven and the earth have feelings and may weep or not weep:

"Neither heaven nor earth shed any tears for them, and they were given no respite." (44:29)

The Prophet, may Allah bless him and grant him peace, said, "There is no jinn or human being or tree or mud or anything within earshot of the voice of the *mu'adhdhin* that will not testify for him

97

on the Day of Rising."

Glory be to Allah! Even trees hear and feel! Even the mud, the small stones, the dry clay! All of them speak! They will speak and testify on the Day of Rising!

> *"Then He directed himself to heaven, when it was smoke, and said to it and to the earth, 'Come willingly or unwillingly.' They both said, 'We come willingly.'"* (41:11)

Allah Almighty says in a *hadith qudsi*, "There is no day when the sun rises but that heaven cries out, 'O Lord, give me permission to fall in pieces on the sons of Adam! They have eaten Your blessing and refused to thank You!' The seas say, 'O Lord, give me permission to drown the sons of Adam. They have eaten Your blessing and refused to thank You!' The earth says, 'O Lord, give me permission to swallow up the sons of Adam! They have eaten Your blessing and refused to thank You!' The mountains say, O Lord, give me permission to crush the sons of Adam! They have eaten Your blessing and refused to thank You!' Allah Almighty says, 'Leave them, leave them. If you had created them, you would have had mercy on them. They are My slaves. If they repent, I will respond to them. If they do not repent, such is their nature.'"

The language of the reckoning

We have already said that all creatures speak and understand one another. Mankind speaks in many languages, so in what language will the slaves be called to account on the Day of Rising?

It may be the language of the Qur'an. It may be Syriac. It may be any language. Allah Almighty, the All-Knowing Protector, has the power to teach His creatures all languages or to speak to them all in one language in which they will be brought to account, giving them instant understanding of it. The important thing is that the Reckoning will be carried out. All creatures will hear and understand every word and every statement on the Day of Rising.

Every veil and covering will be removed by the Will of the All-Merciful.

The Reckoning of the birds and animals

Abu Dharr said that once the Messenger of Allah, may Allah bless him and grant him peace, was sitting when two sheep started fighting and one of them butted the other and made it miscarry. The Messenger of Allah, may Allah bless him and grant him peace, laughed. He was asked, "Why are you laughing, Messenger of Allah?" He said, "I marvel at her. By the One who has My soul in His hand, it will be united with her on the Day of Rising."[1]

Surely that is the summit of justice. On the Day of Rising even a hornless sheep will take it due from a horned sheep which butted it in this world. How much more will that be the case where mankind are concerned!

Abu Dharr reported that the Messenger of Allah, may Allah bless him and grant him peace, passed by two sheep which were butting one another and said, "On the Day of Rising Allah will exact retaliation for this unhorned sheep from the horned one." (al-Qurtubi)

Even inanimate objects will also be questioned on the Day of Rising and retaliation taken for them and from them. It is related that Thabit ibn Tarif asked permission to enter the house of Abu Dharr and heard him raising his voice, saying, "By Allah, were it not for the Day of Disputation, I would hurt you!" Thabit said, "I entered and said, "What is it, Abu Dharr?" He said, "This object. Would you mind hitting it for me?" He said, "By the One Who has the soul of Muhammad in His hand, a sheep will be questioned about why it butted its companion and inanimate objects will asked about why they stubbed a man's toe!" (Ibn Dhahab)

On the Day of Rising, the angels will say to the animals, "Allah Almighty has not gathered you for reward or punishment. He has gathered you to witness the disgrace of the children of Adam." (Qushayri)

The wild beasts and animals will prostrate to Allah. The angels

1. 'Abdullah ibn Ahmad said, "I found this *hadith* in a book belonging to my father in his handwriting.

99

will say, "This is not the day of prostration. This is the day of reward and punishment." The beasts will say, "This is a prostration of thankfulness that Allah did not make us sons of Adam!" (al-Qurtubi)

After the retaliation owed by those creatures to one another is finished, after every one with a due has taken his due, Allah will say to them: "Be dust."

The wild beasts and animals, insects and birds will all be happy and call out. They will call out to people and say, "Praise belongs to Allah! Praise belongs to Allah, sons of Adam, who has not made us like you today! We do not hope for the Garden or fear Hellfire." They will simply be turned to dust.

The unbelievers will weep with terror. They will have nothing but grief and remorse, nothing but sorrow. They will rack their memories for a righteous deed. They will know for certain that this world was only a brief sojourn and that they have not stored up from it any action to help him on this day. That is the implacable reality: they wasted this world and therefore squandered the Next. Remorse will crush them and they will wish that they could save themselves from it, even by becoming non-existent:

"Oh, if only I were dust!" (78:40)

The Questioning of the Messengers

"On the day Allah gathers together the
Messengers and says, 'What response
did you receive?'" (5:109)

The moment of the direct encounter of the Messengers with
their nations has finally arrived. Allah will not call the angels or
Messengers to account: they are protected from sins. Nor will He
call the martyrs to account: their sins were forgiven at the moment
when they were martyred. Allah will assemble the Messengers and
question them. He will question them although, of course, He
knows the answers perfectly well. He will question them in order
to confront all the people who denied the Messengers of Allah and
the *deen* of Allah. He will bring them to confirm to all humanity
that they are in truth noble Messengers who brought them a
Message from Him.

In the presence of all of Allah's creation, human and jinn, and
in the presence of the Celestial Assembly, the All-Kind and
Loving One will say to His noble Messengers:

> *"'What response did you receive?' They will say, 'We*
> *do not know. You are the Knower of all unseen things.'"*

(5:109)

What perfect behaviour! They embody the acme of courtesy
and modesty in the presence of Allah! They are the Messengers of
Allah and they know Him and value Him at His true worth. How
should they claim to have any knowledge, in the presence of the
Knower of all unseen things? The Messengers know outward matters but as for their inward, no one knows them except the Knower

of all unseen things.

The Messengers know about the people from their communities who responded and believed in Allah and those who rejected and did not respond – we seek refuge with Allah! But they do not know those who accepted out of hypocrisy and only for show. Every Messenger knows the extent of the response of his community when he was there among them, but he does not know the extent of the response of his community after they died.

> "But are the Messengers responsible for anything but
> clear transmission?" (16:35)

We must not fail to be guided by the *hadith* of the Messenger of Allah, may Allah bless him and grant him peace, in this respect when he said: "When Allah gathers His slaves on the Day of Rising, the first one to be summoned will be Israfil, peace be upon him. His Lord will say to him, 'What did you do about My Covenant? Did you convey My Covenant?'

"He will say, 'Yes, I conveyed it to Jibril.'

"Jibril, peace be upon him, will be summoned, 'Did Israfil convey My Covenant to you?'

"He will say, 'Yes, Lord, he conveyed it to me.'

"So Israfil will be allowed to go. Then Jibril will be asked, 'Did you convey My Covenant?'

"He will say, 'Yes, I conveyed it to the Messengers.'

"The Messengers will be summoned and He will say, 'Did he convey My Covenant?'

"They will say, 'Yes.'

"Jibril will be allowed to go. Then the Messengers will be asked, 'Did you convey My Covenant?'

"They will say, 'Yes, we conveyed it to our Communities.'

"The communities will be summoned and asked, 'Did My Messengers convey My Covenant?'

"Some of them will affirm and some will deny. The Messengers will say, 'We have witnesses who will testify that we conveyed it.'

"He will say, 'Who will testify for you?'

"They will say, 'Muhammad and his Community.'

"So the Community of Muhammad will be summoned and they will be asked, 'Do you bear witness that My Messengers here conveyed My Covenant those to whom they were sent?'

"They will say, 'Yes, Lord, we testify that they conveyed it.'

"Those communities will say, 'How can they testify against us when they did not meet us?'

"The Lord will say to them, 'How can you testify against people whom you never met?'

"They will say, 'Our Lord, You sent a Messenger to us and sent down Your Covenant and Your Book to us which informed us that they had conveyed it. Therefore we testify to what You gave to us.'

"The Lord will say, 'They have spoken the truth.'"

This *hadith* is confirmed by the words of Allah Almighty:

> *"In this way We have made you a middlemost nation,*
> *so that you could be witnesses against mankind and the*
> *Messenger could be a witness against you."* (2:143)

Ibn An'am said, "It has reached me that the nation who will testify on this day will be the Nation of Muhammad, except for someone who has pity in his heart for his brother." (Ibn al-Mubarak)

Jibril, peace be upon him, brought down a Message from Allah to all the Messengers, a single Message from the One God to all the Messengers: a Message whose basis is *tawhid*, founded on the belief that there is no god but Allah, belief in the Messengers of Allah, and following the Way they were sent to show.

Whenever a Messenger was sent with a Message from Allah to a community, the Messengers before him and their communities were obliged to follow and believe in him. They did not come to abrogate the Message of the Messengers before them but rather to confirm and complete what had come before – until, that is, the time when Muhammad, the Seal of the Messengers, came, and Revelation ceased. Jibril, peace be upon him, will not be sent with a Message to any Messenger after Muhammad, peace and blessings be upon him ever again.

Muhammad and his Community must, therefore, believe in all the prior Messengers, just as the Communities which preceded him must follow him and believe in him. Muhammad was sent with the Qur'an, a Book of knowledge and action from Allah. Allah Almighty recounts to us in the Noble Qur'an the stories of the Prophets and Messengers. All who believe in the oneness of Allah and His Messenger and His Mighty Book believe in all that he brought and believe in all the Messengers and Prophets. The Qur'an will never be exposed to distortion, for the Almighty says of it:

> "It is We Who have sent down the Remembrance and truly We are its Preservers." (15:9)

The Community of Muhammad believes in this Book and is completely certain about everything in it. It is the Community which testifies to all the Messengers and Prophets since the time of Adam until the Seal of the Messenger through the pages of the Immense Qur'an. It is the Community which believes in all the Messengers without favouring any of them over the others. This Community deserves, indeed the believers in it are obliged, to become witnesses against people on the Day of Reckoning. The Messenger who was sent with this Qur'an is obliged to be a witness against all of them.

> "That Day We will raise up among every Community a witness against them from amongst themselves and bring you as a witness against them. We have revealed the Book to you making all things clear and as guidance and mercy and good news for the Muslims." (16:89)

> "Is it other than the deen of Allah that you desire, when everything in the heavens and earth submits to Him, willingly or unwillingly, and you will be returned to Him? Say, 'We believe in Allah and what has been revealed to us and what was revealed to Ibrahim and Isma'il and Ishaq and Ya'qub and the Tribes, and what Musa and 'Isa and all the Prophets were given by their Lord. We do not dif-

ferentiate between any of them. We are Muslims who submit to Him.' Whoever desires other than Islam as deen, *it will not be accepted from him, and in the Next World he will be one of the losers.*" (3:83-85)

Everyone will be with what
he worshipped

*"On the day We gather them all together, We shall
then say to those who attributed partners to Allah, 'To
your place, you and your partner-gods!'"* **(10:28)**

What a fearsome and terrible fate! On the Day of Rising, a
strong, compelling voice will proclaim: "Let every Community
follow what it worshipped." People will separate and everyone
will follow what they worshipped. Every Community will stand
with the gods they worshipped in this world instead of Allah,
whether that was angels, a human beings, a jinn, an animal, or
inanimate objects.

The so-called 'god' which was itself a created being will stand
there in front of them and they will stand behind it. Human beings
and jinn will no longer have any will of their own. A person will
have no power over his limbs, which will be under the direct command of their Creator. People will have no power over their feet,
which will take them along in spite of their desire to the contrary.
They will take them to whatever or whoever they worshipped in
this world. The idolaters will have no power to deceive. No one
will be able to stand in any other place than his own. He will not
be able to stand with a god other than the one which he worshipped in this world.

When the call is heard, idolaters will hasten to the stones
which they made and worshipped and stand behind them. People
who worshipped gold statues, like the Buddhists, will go to their
idols to seek their protection. People who worshipped the sun,
moon, stars and planets will be gathered together in groups and

each group will be placed behind what it worshipped. Those who worshipped animals, like the Hindus, will go to the animals they worshipped and stand behind them. Human beings will find themselves behind a cow or whatever other animal they held sacred. People such as sorcerers who worshipped the jinn and devils will go to their devils. People who worshipped their fathers or their leaders will be gathered behind those whom they worshipped. The people of Pharaoh will stand behind Pharaoh.

People who worshipped 'Uzayr will go to Shaytan, who inspired them to do so and who will appear in the form of 'Uzayr, which they will follow. It will be the same for those who worshipped 'Isa son of Maryam. All who associated something with the Creator and worshipped one of His creatures will follow whatever they worshipped before until none are left except those who worshipped the True Creator and Provider alone. They will be gathered together.

Then the Resurrector and Reckoner will bring together the idolaters and say to them, "To your place, you and your partner-gods!" No one will be able to move from their place. How humiliating it will be! Those are the 'gods' they made with their hands and their imaginations: People will find that they have no power whatsoever. Hearts will quake and bodies will tremble. Each will remain in his place. There will be no movement or whisper. Then the Command of Allah will come and separate the idolaters from their partner-gods, cutting the connection between them. Allah says:

"Then We shall sift them out." (10:28)

Muslim reported that some people asked the Messenger of Allah, may Allah bless him and grant him peace, "Messenger of Allah, will we see our Lord on the Day of Rising?"

The Messenger of Allah, may Allah bless him and grant him peace, asked them, "Do you have any difficulty in seeing the moon on the night when it is full?'"

"No, Messenger of Allah."

"Do you have in difficulty in seeing the light of the sun when there is no cloud in front of it?"

"No," they replied.

"That is how you will see Him," he said. "Allah will gather people on the Day of Rising and say, 'Whoever worshipped anything, let him follow it.' Those who worshipped the sun will follow the sun. Those who worshipped the moon will follow the moon. Those who worshipped idols will follow their idols. This Community will be left there along with its hypocrites. Allah will come to them in a form which they do not recognise and will say, 'I am your Lord.' They will say, 'We seek refuge with Allah. We are here until our Lord comes to us.' When our Lord comes, we will recognise Him.' Then Allah will come to them in a form which they do recognise, and will say, 'I am your Lord.' They will follow Him.

"The *Sirat* will be set up over Jahannam, and I and my Community will be the first to cross. On that Day none but the Messengers will speak and the prayer of the Messengers on that day will be, 'O Allah, safety, safety!' In Jahannam there will be pronged flesh-hooks like the thorns of the *sa'dan*[1] plant. Have you seen the *sa'dan*?" "Yes, Messenger of Allah," they replied. He said, "They are like *sa'dan* thorns, but only Allah knows their immense size. They will snag people according to their actions. Some people will be barred by their actions and some will cross and so escape..."

Then the Confrontation will begin: the confrontation between the idolaters and their gods. Some creatures were worshipped without their incurring any sin – creatures with no will of their own. They do not have any power to mislead anyone into worshipping them. They were created naturally worshipping Allah and glorifying Him: things like the sun, moon, stars, planets, fire, stones, and animals. No sin can be imputed to created things such as these.

There are also human beings who do have will but who were worshipped against their will after they left this world without any desire or knowledge on their part, such as 'Isa, peace be upon him, his mother Maryam, and 'Uzayr. They are among the best of

---

1. The name of a plant with a prickly head on which camels pasture. If you step on one of its thorns, it winds around your foot.

Allah's creation and certainly have no part in the abominable crime that is ascribed to them.

The same applies to the angels who were worshipped instead of Allah even though Allah essentially created them to obey Him and they are bound by the commands of the Almighty. The angels are messengers of Allah to His slaves with the truth. How can they be worshipped? Allah will not call those innocent beings to account and will not punish them. Instead, they will be asked to confront those who worshipped them and the ignominy of those people will be laid bare to the entire assembly.

The "gods" who sinned will be those shaytans of men and jinn who called on people to worship them and who misled them. Indeed some of them, such as Pharaoh, even compelled people to worship them by force. Those are the ones who deserve a harsh reckoning and will be rewarded with the severest punishment.

Those who were taken as gods instead of Allah or together with Allah will feel great fear! They will be frightened of the terror of the Standing. In their weakness they will seek refuge in the True God, their All-Watchful Creator, trying to exonerate themselves from the terrible charges they face. They will testify to Allah and declare that they had no knowledge of the divine status which their followers ascribed to them.

> *"Their partner-gods will say, 'It was not us you worshipped. Allah is sufficient witness between us and you. We were unmindful of your worship.'"* (10:28-29)

The questioning of the angels

"The day We gather all of them together and then say to the angels, 'Was it you that these people were worshipping?' they will say, 'Glory be to You!'" You are All-Exalted and All-Pure. You are All-Blessed. None but You is worthy of worship! *"You are our Protector from them."* We are Your slaves and we declare ourselves innocent of what they did. *"No, they were worshipping the jinn. Most of them believed in them."* (34:41) "They were not wor-

109

shipping us at all but rather shaytans of the jinn who inspired them to worship other than You. O Lord, we did not mislead anyone into worshipping us. We did not know anything about it. We do not possess any power to disobey You. We glorify You night and day."

Allah knows that the angels *"do not disobey Allah in whatever He commands them to do and they do as they are commanded."* (66:6)

The questioning of 'Isa, peace be upon him

"And when Allah says, 'O 'Isa son of Maryam! Did you tell people, "Take me and my mother as two gods besides Allah"?'" (5:116)

Allah Almighty does not really intend this question to be directed to 'Isa son of Maryam, for He knows very well what he said to people. It is intended for those who worshipped 'Isa. How should it be possible for him to lay claim to divinity when he knows that he is one of the servants of Allah, a righteous Prophet among the best of Allah's creation? 'Isa will hasten to declare himself innocent of that crime, of which even an ordinary Muslim would be incapable, let alone a noble Messenger.

'Isa will quake and will pray humbly to his Lord. He will hasten to declare Him exalted beyond there being anything worthy of worship but Him, demonstrating belief and humility:

"He will say, 'Glory be to You! It is not for me to say what I have no right to say! If I did say it, then You know it. You know what is in my soul but I do not know what is in Your Self. Truly You are the Knower of all unseen things.'" (5:116)

'Isa will proclaim before the assembly his servantship to Allah alone with no partner.

> *"I told them nothing but what You ordered me to say:*
> *'Worship Allah, my Lord and your Lord.'"* (5:117)

No one worshipped 'Isa during the time he was in this world. They worshipped him and spread statements about him after he had risen to the Next World. He was responsible for them while he was among them but his responsibility ended when he left. He entrusted their affair to Allah Almighty.

> *"I was a witness concerning them as long so I remained among them, but when You took me back to You, You were the Watcher over them. You are Witness of all things. If You punish them, they are Your slaves. If you forgive them, You are the Almighty, the All-Wise."* (5:117)

The judgement of Allah will ensue and a decisive refutation will be made by 'Isa, peace be upon him, in which he refuses to have anything to do with the lies told about him or the liars who told them. He will have nothing to do with those who worshipped anything other than Allah – glory be to Him and may He exalted! The judgement of Allah will be given.

> *"Allah will say, 'This is the Day when the truthfulness of the truthful will benefit them. They shall have Gardens with rivers flowing under them, remaining in them timelessly, forever without end. Allah is pleased with them and they are pleased with Him. That is the Great Triumph.' The kingdom of the heavens and the earth and everything in them belongs to Allah. He has power over all things."*

(5:119-120)

The questioning of everything that was worshipped besides Allah

Allah Almighty will bring the sun, the moon, the stars, the

planets and the stones and anything that was worshipped instead of Him and ask each of them whether they had told people to worship them instead of Allah in order to rebuke those who worshipped them. They will be terrified and they will speak, all of them declaring themselves innocent of that terrible accusation: "Glory be to You! You are our Master, and we are subjected to You, not to them. We glorify You night and day. We are compelled to obey You and worship You. How could we ask them to worship us? We disdain them. We wish we could annihilate them. We are innocent of them. *"When those who were followed disown those who followed…"* (2:166)

Allah will question those creatures although He knows everything about them: *"There is nothing which does not glorify His praise."* (17:44)

The confrontation of the Shaytans with their worshippers

The shaytans will deny all responsibility for those who worshipped them, abandoning them completely. They will not deny that they rejected Allah. They will not deny that they misled those people to attribute partners to Allah Almighty. But they will deny that they compelled them to do it. They may have had power over their bodies but their power did not extend to their hearts or to their belief. It was not possible for their power to reach the soul even if they wanted it to.

Those shaytans will stand before Allah with audacity and say:

"…Our Lord, those people who we misled, we only misled them as we ourselves were misled. We declare to You our innocence. It was not us that they were worshipping!" (28:63)

Their worshippers will look to them for help – but in vain!

"They will call on them but they will not respond to them. And they will see the punishment. If only they had

112

been guided!" (28:64)

What disgrace and shame! Those they thought would help them on that dreadful Day simply wash their hands of them. If only they had remembered the position of Iblis, the leader of the shaytans of men and jinn! If only they had remembered his aggressive stance when he proclaimed his enmity to Adam and all his descendants!

"He said, 'By Your might, I will mislead all of them except for Your chosen slaves among them.'" (38:82-83)

If only they had thought about that! If only they had avoided him in this world and not allowed him to divert them from the truth.

"The day when He summons them and says, 'How did you respond to the Messengers?' On that day the facts will be made obscure for them and they will not be able to question one another." (28:65-66)

On that day the idolaters will have no answers. At first they will take refuge in silence and then after their true nature has been revealed they will deny themselves. They will feel nothing but shame and humiliation. They will try to repudiate their past and all their evil actions. They will pretend to forget that they attributed partners to Allah in their life in this world. They will affirm His Oneness – glory be to Him and may He be exalted! But it will be too late.

"The Day We gather them all together We will say to those who worshipped others besides Allah: 'Where are your partner-gods, those for whom you made such claims?' Then they will have no other recourse than to say, 'By Allah, our Lord, We were not idolaters.' See how they lie against themselves and how what they were fabricating has forsaken them!" (6:24-25)

"Say: 'Who provides for you out of heaven and earth? Who has control over hearing and sight? Who brings forth

113

the living from the dead and the dead from the living?
Who directs the affair?' They will say, 'Allah.' So say,
'Will you not then be godfearing?' That is Allah, your
Lord, the Truth; and what is there after truth except mis-
guidance? So how have you been distracted? Thus is the
word of your Lord realised against those who are wanton-
ly deviant in that they do not believe. Say: 'Can any of
your partner-gods originate creation and then bring it
back again?' Say: 'Allah originates creation and then will
bring it back again. So how have you been perverted?'
Say: 'Can any of your partner-gods guide to the truth?'
Say: 'Allah guides to the truth. Who has more right to be
followed – He Who guides to the truth, or he who cannot
guide unless he is guided? What is wrong with you? How
do you reach your judgement?' Most of them follow noth-
ing but conjecture. Conjecture is of no avail at all against
the truth. Allah certainly knows what they are doing."

(10:31-36)

The Book and the Preserved Tablet

"What is this Book which does not pass over any action, small or great, without recording it?..." (18:49)

This matter is the subject of many questions. What is the Preserved Tablet? What is the Book? What is the connection between them? How can a book record every small and great action which a human does? What is the natural form we were created on? How did Allah make us bear witness to His sovereignty? Where were we at that time?

Patience, patience! The questions are many but the knowledge of Allah is more abundant. We will attempt together to glean some snatches which He has bestowed on us from His overflowing fount of inexhaustible knowledge. Call on Allah with me to give us success in what will make Him pleased with us and to put us far from what will make Him angry with us and to grant an opening to us. May He accept our actions and record His acceptance of them in Heaven and earth and put all of them in the balance of our reckoning.

The Decree on the Preserved Tablet

The All-Holy King existed from before time and will continue to exist after time. He created the Preserved Tablet. He created the Pen and said to it, "Write!" and the Pen wrote. It wrote the Decree. 'Ubada ibn as-Samit reported that he heard the Messenger of Allah, may Allah bless him and grant him peace, say, "The first thing Allah created was the Pen. He said to it, 'Write,' and it said, 'What shall I write?' He said, 'Write the Decree.' It wrote what was and what will be until the end of time." (Abu Dawud, at-Tirmidhi and Ahmad)

115

Ibn 'Abbas reported that the Messenger of Allah, may Allah bless him and grant him peace, said, "Allah Almighty created a Preserved Tablet from white pearl with pages of red ruby whose pen is of light and whose writing is of light." (at-Tabarani) According to the *Sahih* of Muslim, the Messenger of Allah, may Allah bless him and grant him peace, said, "Allah wrote the decrees of creation fifty thousand years before He created the heavens and the earth."

He did not create existence by chance or haphazardly. He did not create it to no purpose. The destinies of every creature were already in the pre-eternal knowledge of Allah. He determined them by far-reaching wisdom and with the utmost precision. He determined them in a precise order and with complete harmony. Then they were inscribed in the Mother of the Book, the Preserved Tablet. Then Allah created existence, creating the heavens and the earth and all the creatures in them; and He created mankind. Do not imagine that the Preserved Tablet is a book confined merely to the history of your life. You are not the sole creature in existence.

The Preserved Tablet is a comprehensive and complete book. It is a record full of knowledge and information: the knowledge of the Unseen, the knowledge of all religions, the Divine Books, the Noble Qur'an. *"It truly is a Noble Qur'an in a closely guarded Book."* (56:77-78) *"We have made it an Arabic Qur'an so that hopefully you might use your understanding. It is in the Mother of the Book with Us, sublime, full of wisdom."* (43:3-4) *"It is indeed a Glorious Qur'an on a Preserved Tablet."* (85:21-22)

Everything is there: astronomy, physics, chemistry, mathematics, geography, biology, medicine, engineering, and other knowledges which are beyond number, knowledges of which human knowledge will never comprise more than the smallest fraction. The furthest that a human being as an individual can reach is his specialisation in a minute part of a minute part of just one of the branches of one of the knowledges which cannot be numbered belonging to the All-Vast, the All-Knowing – may His majesty be exalted and His names hallowed! The whole of human knowledge from the beginning of creation until today is no more than the tiniest fraction of the pre-eternal knowledge of Allah.

"All things We have created in due measure." (54:49) The All-Knowing, All-Wise created everything in due measure. He created the vast world of space. There are galaxies and gigantic celestial bodies swimming in immeasurable orbits, and billions of stars and planets, some of which are visible and some of which cannot be seen with the naked eye. Some of them cannot even be seen with telescopes and instruments. They are sensed rather than seen. Some of them are still beyond the knowledge of astronomers. Every star swims in its gravitational field which is not near the gravitational field of another star so that there is no conflict.

Glory be to Allah! He determined the mass of the sun, the degree of its heat and its distance from the earth. He determined the mass of the earth, the speed of its revolution on its axis, its orbit around the sun, the distance of the moon from it and the speed of the moon's orbit around the earth. He took everything into consideration and fixed its position and its distances in relation to all that is around it and the extent of its effect in the universe.

Glory be to Allah! He determined the proportions of the distribution of moisture and dryness in the earth. He determined its layers. He determined the proportions of the elements of water and air to be exactly what is necessary for life on its surface to exist. And millions of other relationships which are so fine that if there were any discrepancy anywhere, everything would change and it would be the absolute end of life on the surface of the earth. *"...The Knower of the Unseen, Whom not even the weight of the smallest particle eludes, in the heavens or in the earth. Nor is there anything smaller than that, or larger, which is not in a Clear Record."* (34:3)

Glory be to the All-Powerful Determiner! He created every atom with an exact weight so that it can precisely perform its unique role in the scheme of things. He created what is even smaller than atoms: protons, electrons and neutrons. The smallest atom is the atom of the gas of light hydrogen at whose centre is a proton with a positive electric charge. Revolving around it is a body smaller than it - an electron with a negative charge. There are atoms which are more complex than the simple hydrogen atom and have neutrons at their centre which have no charge. The most complex atom is uranium which contains 92 electrons, 92 protons and 146 neutrons.

Each element consists of atoms of the same kind since one element differs from another by the difference of the number of protons in the nucleus of their atoms. Molecules are formed from elements and matter consists of masses of molecules. When one atom of oxygen bonds with two atoms of hydrogen, a water molecule is formed. What Divine Greatness beyond any limits! What precision in determination and perfection of management! What vast, immense pre-eternal knowledge! And this is merely an infinitesimal part of what is inscribed on the Preserved Tablet.

Just pause for a minute and think about these lines. Where are they in relation to the great store of human knowledge, the knowledge to which the mind of man has attained from the beginning of creation until today? And where is all that human knowledge in relation to the pre-eternal knowledge of Allah? It is beyond any possible description that could be applied to it. These lines are like a small electron revolving around the nucleus of one of the atoms of the earth. The whole of human knowledge might correspond to the earth. The entire universe on that scale would not be sufficient to contain the knowledge of the Tablet. Glory be to You, O Allah!

What shall I say about the determination of the creation of inanimates and plants, microbes and insects? What about all the birds and animals? The amoeba – that tiny animal of a single cell, which can move and eat and exhibit every sign of life. I must say, and you must say with me: Glory be to Allah! Allah is the One who determined the immense currents of history in the same way that He determines the effect of each breath in the chest of every tiny creature. He determined everything in existence. He set up balance and harmony between all.

Glory be to the Creator and Fashioner! He created man. He designed the human body and the millions of cells it contains, the red corpuscles, the white corpuscles, the lymph glands, the brain cells, the heart, the lungs, the kidneys, the liver and all the other cells which combine to form limbs and systems, each of which has a predetermined function and role in preserving the health and life of man. The systems are concealed inside a large skeleton consisting of more than 200 bones, held together by ligaments whose ends are covered with cartilage. There are more than 500 muscles in the human body, each of which is formed of thousands of fibres. The large skeleton in turn is covered with flesh which is covered by a layer of skin.

Glory be to the Ever-Reliable Guide! He did not confine His design to the creation of the body but extended it through time. It includes every breath which emerges from a man's lungs. He determined his provision, actions, life-span, and his eternal bliss or damnation. He determined the extent of his effect as an individual on existence as a whole, something which even the person himself does not know; but it is all inscribed on the Preserved Tablet in the pre-eternal knowledge of the Great Creator – may His majesty be exalted and His names hallowed.

"Nothing happens, either in the earth or in yourselves, but that it is in a Book before We bring it into being. That is easy for Allah, so that you may not be grieved about the things that pass you by or exult about the things that come to you. Allah does not love any vain or boastful man." (57:22-23)

I like what 'Ikrima, may Allah be pleased with him, said about this *ayat*: "There is no one who does not feel joy and sorrow; but turn your joy to thankfulness and your sorrow to steadfastness."

No human being is created without purpose. No event occurs in your life except by a predetermined wisdom which you may or may not perceive as time goes by. Your perception is limited because your life is limited. The pre-eternal and post-temporal knowledge of Allah is absolute without limits. So let your heart be at peace in His power – glory be to Him and may He be exalted – because He is aware of what you do not see.

Often events repeat themselves throughout the course of human life, such as emigration from one land to another, childlessness, or having children late in life. What is the wisdom behind the occurrence of those events and others? The wisdom varies according to the time, place, and individual.

119

Ibrahim, peace and blessings be upon him, the father of the Prophets, is an excellent example. He emigrated from Babylon to Greater Syria and travelled to Egypt and to the Hijaz. When he arrived in Egypt, his wife Sara was barren and had not given birth to any children. They were already old. They received the gift of Hajar, the Egyptian Copt, and she returned with them to Syria. Ibrahim married her and she bore him Isma'il, peace be upon him, who was the father of the Arabs. Hajar settled and nursed Isma'il in Makka near the Sacred House of Allah. Centuries passed until Muhammad, peace and blessings be upon him, was born in Makka at the Sacred House of Allah, grew up there and bore the Message of Islam to the entire world and was the Seal of the Prophets.

When Ibrahim emigrated to Syria, he had only one child. Then Allah gave him Ishaq thirteen years after the birth of Isma'il. Allah made Ishaq the progenitor of many righteous Prophets and placed Prophethood and the Book among his descendants. Syria and the Hijaz became the fount of the Divine Religions as He had predetermined in His pre-eternal knowledge. Time continued and events took place which continue to affect the course of the life of the entire world until today.

> *"The keys of the Unseen are in His possession. No one knows them except Him. He knows everything in the land and sea. Not a leaf falls without His knowing it. There is no seed in the darkness of the earth, and nothing wet thing or dry that is not in a Clear Book."* (6:59)

Glory be to Allah! He determined everything in existence. Every leaf on every tree which falls to earth is numbered and known in the pre-eternal knowledge of Allah, determined and recorded in the Preserved Tablet; every single grain of dust, the dust of the earth which man disdains yet which was the source of his physical existence, is recorded. There is no element in our body which does not correspond to one of the elements of our mother, the earth.

Glory be to Allah! There is also the essence of the human being: the Divine secret which Allah entrusted to him. It is the spirit. The All-Holy King breathed some of His Pure Spirit into the clay body of Adam and in him it became a torch lit from the Light of Allah. He accepted the contract in his natural form. He carried the trust, descended to earth and became the greatest creature on its surface. He became Allah's regent on the earth. All creatures were created for His sake. But despite that, however much the human intellect tries to explore the horizons of knowledge, it continues to swim in a vast sea of the unknown – the unknown which is known only to Allah.

The Primal Contract of Mankind

"When your Lord took all their descendants from the loins of the children of Adam..." (7:172)

When Adam was created, all of his descendants were created in his back.[1] At that time the children of Adam were mere atoms so incredibly minute that they could not seen by the naked eye. Every atom of the descendants of Adam contained the whole life of its owner, his attributes and his life history. Every man who is born contains his descendants in his back; and the reverse is true since the life of every man is hidden in his father's back. Thus generations will succeed one another until the Last Hour comes.

That is how we existed in the *Malakut* when Allah made His primal contract with us, the contract of *tawhid*. It is a covenant contracted between mankind in its natural state at its inception and the Creator of mankind.

The Messenger of Allah, may Allah bless him and grant him peace, said, "Allah stroked the back of Adam and brought forth from it the progeny stored in it: everyone who will come into existence up until the Last Hour. He said to them, 'Am I not your Lord?' They replied, 'Yes, You are our Lord - glory be to You!'" Every soul which would come into being until the Day of Rising answered its Creator, affirming and acknowledging His lordship and its slavehood to Him – glory be to Him and may He be exalted! All testified to His Oneness when they were merely scattered atoms collected in the hand of the All-Majestic: *"They said, 'Yes indeed; we bear witness!'"* (7:172)

In the two *Sahih* collections, Abu Hurayra, may Allah be pleased with him, reported that the Messenger of Allah, may Allah bless him and grant him peace, said, "Every child is born in the

---

1. See the note on page 30.

122

natural form." The natural form is established in every living cell from its original formation. The Immense Creator lodged it in the being of man from the time he was in the world of atoms. They have no justification for later breaking the contract established between them and their Creator. That contract has its consequences:

> *"Lest you say on the Day of Rising, 'We were unaware of this.' Or lest you say, 'Our forefathers attributed partners to Allah before our time, and we are merely descendants coming after them. Will You then destroy us for what those falsifiers did?'"* (7:172-173)

Allah instilled the natural form in man and gave him intelligence. But the Almighty knew that the natural form would deviate and that the intellect would go astray. In the *Sahih* of Muslim, 'Iyad ibn Himar reported that the Messenger of Allah said, may Allah bless him and grant him peace: "Allah says, 'I created My slaves as natural believers (*hanif*), and then the shaytans went to them and led them astray from their *deen* and made unlawful for them what was lawful for them."

Poor man! He swiftly drowned in the sea of forgetfulness and lost himself, even though his safety lay in the simplest of procedures. In the *Sahih* of al-Bukhari we find: "Allah will ask the person with the least punishment among the people of the Fire: 'If you had everything in the earth, would you ransom yourself with it?' He will say, 'Yes.' He will say, 'I asked you for something much easier than that when you were in the loins of Adam: not to associate anyone else with Me. Yet in spite of that you refused anything but idolatry.'" (Reported from Anas)

The mercy of Allah Almighty has decided that His slaves will not be called to account for the primal contract. They will not be called to account for the intellect which He bestowed on them. They will only be called to account after the Messengers have been sent among them to remind them, warn them and give them good news. After that people will have no argument. Glory be to You, O Allah! O All-Merciful! O All-Compassionate!

"That is how We make the signs distinct so that perhaps they will return." (7:174)

"Anyone who is guided is guided only for his own good. Anyone who is misguided is only misguided to his detriment. No bearer of a burden can bear that of another. We never punish until We have sent a Messenger." (17:15)

The Book and the Noble Scribes

Every man will also have his own personal book which will be opened, a book in which the whole history of his life is written down from birth to death. That book will contain every detail as foreordained in the pre-eternal knowledge of Allah. It is simply the specific text of what is inscribed on the Preserved Tablet concerning the life of the individual in question. This tells us the provenance of the book; but we still need to know when it will be opened, how it is written, when it will be given, and how and when it tells us the truth about our lives.

Rays of light emanate from the Noble Qur'an, a light which guides us to the stages of the creation of man leading up to his birth, then through to his death, and then his resurrection on the Day of Resurrection. The Majestic Qur'an gives us the complete story with the utmost splendour, concision and clarity of expression, a knowledge which has only become part of human knowledge after aeons of human history. The Immense Qur'an summarises it for us in five *ayats* of *Surat al-Mu'minin*:

> "*We created man from the purest kind of clay; then made him a drop in a secure receptacle; then created the drop into a clot and created the clot into a lump and created the lump into bones and clothed the bones in flesh; and then brought him into being as another creature. So Blessed be Allah, the Best of Creators! Then subsequently you will most surely die. Then on the Day of Rising you will be raised again.*" (23:12-16)

Glory be to Allah! Clay was transformed into living cells which became man. What an awesome disparity there is between mud and man! A distance which contains within it an immense secret: the secret of life. The book of man is opened in those first stages of his creation, even before his formation is complete, as a foetus in his mother's womb, when the life-force is breathed into him.

125

It is recorded in the *Sahih* collections that Ibn Mas'ud reported that the Messenger of Allah, may Allah bless him and grant him peace, said, "The way that each of you is created is that you are gathered in your mother's womb for forty days as a sperm-drop and then for a similar length of time as a blood-clot and then for a similar length of time as a lump of flesh. Then an angel is sent and breathes the spirit (*ruh*) into you and is encharged with four commandments: to write down your provision, your life-span, your actions, and whether you will be happy or damned in the Afterlife."

The creation of man is completed and then he emerges into the world and he emerges free, enjoying complete liberty in his intention and consciousness, and in his secret. He can do whatever he wishes but he is not left unobserved. Beware, O man, beware! You are not alone. *"Standing over you are guardians, noble, recording. They know everything you do."* (82:10-12) O child of Adam, be ashamed before the noble scribes. At your right hand there is an angel who writes down all your good needs and at your left another who writes down your evil deeds. You know that and yet you do not live as if you were conscious of it. The early Muslims knew it and lived in recognition of it with belief and complete certainty. It is even related that Imam Ahmad ibn Hanbal moaned when he was ill but that when he heard that moans are recorded he was silent until he died, may Allah be pleased with him. I can only remain silent on this point. Let the Noble Qur'an speak; let the noble *hadith* explain; and let the scholars clarify their words.

> *"We created man and We know what his own self whispers to him, and We are nearer to him than his jugular vein. And the two recording angels are recording, sitting one on the right and one on the left. He does not utter a single word without a watcher by him ready at hand. The throes of death come exposing the truth. That is what you were trying to evade! The Trumpet will be blown. That is the Day of the Threat. Every soul comes together with a driver and a witness: 'You were heedless of this. Therefore We have removed from you your covering and so today your eyesight is sharp.'"* (50:16-22)

Imam Ahmad related from 'Alqama from Bilal ibn al-Harith al-Muzani, may Allah be pleased with him, that the Messenger of Allah, may Allah bless him and grant him peace, stated, "A man may say something which pleases Allah Almighty without him realising the full extent of its implication and because of it, Allah prescribes His pleasure for him until the Day he meets Him. And a man may likewise say something which angers Allah Almighty without him realising the full extent of its implication and because of it, Allah prescribes His wrath for him until the Day he meets Him." 'Alqama used to say, "How many words I am forbidden by the *hadith* of Bilal ibn al-Harith!"

Al-Ahnaf ibn Qays said "The one on the right records good actions and he has authority over the one on the left. If someone commits an error, he says, 'Wait.' If he asks Allah to forgive him, he forbids him to record it. If he refuses to ask forgiveness, then he records it." Ibn Abi Hatim related that.

Explaining the *ayat "sitting one on the right and one on the left,"* al-Hasan al-Basri said, "O son of Adam, a page is unrolled for you and two noble angels are entrusted to you. One of them is on your right and the other on your left. The one on your right records your good actions and the one on your left records your bad actions. So do what you wish, a little or much. When you die, your page is rolled up and placed with you on your neck in your grave until you emerge on the Day of Resurrection. About that, the Almighty says, *'We have fastened the destiny of every man about his neck and on the Day of Rising We will bring out a book for him which he will find spread open in front of him. "Read your book! Today your own self is reckoner enough against you!"'"* (17:13-14) Then he said, "Act with justice. Allah is the One who made you a self-reckoner."

'Ali ibn Abi Talha reported that Ibn 'Abbas, may Allah be pleased with him and his father, said about Allah's words: *"He does not utter a single word, without a watcher by him ready at hand."* He writes down all the good or evil things the man says or does, even writing down the actual words, 'I ate, I drank, I went, I came, I saw.' Every Thursday he presents his words and actions, and the good or evil in them is registered and the rest discarded.

127

That is confirmed by His words: *'Allah obliterates whatever He wills or confirms it. The Mother of the Book is with Him.'"* (13:39) O son of Adam! Be ashamed before the Noble Recorders who guard you night and day!

> *"It makes no difference whether you keep secret what you say or voice it out loud, whether you hide in the night or go out in the day. Each person has a succession of angels in front of him and behind him, guarding him by Allah's command. Allah never changes a people's state unless they change what is in themselves..."* (13:10-11)

We find in the two *Sahih* collections, in *hadiths* from Abu Hurayra, that the Prophet, may Allah bless him and grant him peace, said, "There are angels which take turns in being with you in the night with other angels in the day and they meet together at the prayers of *Fajr* and *'Asr*. Then those who were with you during the night ascend and their Lord asks them – although He knows you better than them – 'How were My slaves when you left them?' They say, 'When we left them they were praying, and when we came to them they were praying.'"

'Ikrima reported that Ibn 'Abbas said about *"guarding him by Allah's command"*: "The angels guard him before and behind him. When the decree of Allah comes, they leave him."

Mujahid said, "There is no one who does not have an angel charged with guarding him in his sleep and while he is awake from jinn, men and reptiles. None of those things come to him without the angel saying to him, 'Watch out behind you!' unless it is something which Allah has given leave to afflict him."

Imam Ahmad reported from 'Abdullah that the Messenger of Allah, may Allah bless him and grant him peace, said, "There is not one of you who does not have a companion of the jinn entrusted to him as well as a companion of the angels." They asked, "Even you, Messenger of Allah?" He replied, "Even I, but Allah helped me against him, and he only commands me to do good."

Al-Bukhari reported from Abu Hurayra that the Messenger of Allah said, may Allah bless him and grant him peace: "The group prayer is twenty-five degrees more excellent than the prayer alone. The angels of the night and the angels of the day meet at the *Fajr* prayer." According to the *Sahih* of Muslim Abu Hurayra reported that the Messenger of Allah, may Allah bless him and grant him peace, was asked, "Which is the best prayer after the prescribed one?" He replied, "The night prayer (*tahajjud*)."

It is affirmed in the *Sahih* collections and elsewhere from a group of Companions, may Allah be pleased with all of them, that the Messenger of Allah, may Allah bless him and grant him peace, said. "Allah Almighty descends every night to the lowest heaven, when the final third of the night remains and says, 'Is there anyone who repents, so I may turn to him? Is there anyone who asks for-giveness, so that I may forgive him? Is there anyone who asks, so that I may grant him his request?' until dawn rises."

It is confirmed in the *Sahih* that the Messenger of Allah, may Allah bless him and grant him peace, told Jibril when he asked him about *ihsan:* "It is that you worship Allah as if you saw Him. If you do not see Him, He sees you."

In the *Sahih*, "The actions of the night rise to Him before day-break and the actions of the day before nightfall."

Anas ibn Malik reported that the Prophet, may Allah bless him and grant him peace, said, "If any two guardian angels of the night or day ascend with what they have recorded and Allah finds good on the first page and the last page, Allah Almighty says, 'I call on you to bear witness that I have forgiven My slave for what is between the two end pages." (at-Tirmidhi)

Anas ibn Malik reported that the Prophet said, may Allah bless him and grant him peace: "There is no person who does not have two gates in heaven: a gate from which his provision emerges and a gate by which his actions and words enter. When he dies, they miss him and weep for him." He recited this *ayat: "Neither heav-en nor earth shed any tears for them"* (44:29). He went on, "That is because they did not do any righteous actions on the earth to cause it to weep for them, and no good words or righteous actions rose from them to heaven so that it should miss them and weep for them." (Abu Ya'la)

129

Shurayh ibn 'Ubayd al-Khadrami said that the Messenger of Allah, may Allah bless him and grant him peace, said, "Islam began as a stranger and will revert to being a stranger as it began. There is no exile for the believer. No believer dies in exile absent from those who would weep for him without heaven and earth weeping for him." Then the Messenger of Allah, may Allah bless him and grant him peace, recited: *"Neither heaven nor earth shed any tears for them"* (44:29), and added, "They do not weep for an unbeliever." (Ibn Jarir)

A man went to Ibn 'Abbas, may Allah be pleased with him and his father, and asked, "Abu'l-'Abbas! What do you think of the words of Allah Almighty, *'Neither heaven nor earth shed any tears for them and they were given no respite'* (44:29)? Do heaven and earth weep for people?" He replied, "There is no creature which does not have a gate in heaven from which his provision descends and through which his actions ascend. When a believer dies the gate through which his actions used to ascend and from which his provision used to descend is closed and it misses him and weeps for him. When the place on the earth where he used to pray and remember Allah Almighty misses him it also weeps. The people of Pharaoh do not have any righteous traces in the earth and no good ascended to Allah Almighty from them and so the heaven and earth did not weep for them." (Ibn Jarir)

How should the earth not weep for a slave who used to make it flourish with bowing and prostration? Why should heaven not weep for a slave whose *takbir* and glorification in it hummed like the humming of a bee? *"All good words ascend to Him and He lifts up all righteous deeds..."* (35:10)

Imam Ahmad related from an-Nu'man ibn Bashir that the Messenger of Allah, may Allah bless him and grant him peace, said, "Those who remember Allah Almighty with glorification, *takbir*, praise and proclaiming His Unity are close to one another around the Throne. There is a humming sound like the humming of bees which marks out those who did the invocation. Would you not like to have something distinguishing you in the Presence of Allah?"

Ibn Abi Hatim reported from Ja'far ibn Muhammad that he heard his father say, "The Messenger of Allah, may Allah bless him and grant him peace, looked at the Angel of Death standing at the head of one of the Ansar. The Prophet, may Allah bless him and grant him peace, said to him, 'Angel of Death, be gentle to my Companion. He is a believer.' The Angel of Death replied, 'Muhammad, be of good cheer and delight. I am gentle to every believer. Know that there is no mud hut or tent anywhere on earth which I do not examine five times every day so that I know their young and old better than they do themselves. By Allah, O Muhammad, if I wanted to take the soul of a gnat, I would not be able to do that without Allah commanding me to take it."

Man receives a brand of the Light of Allah and accepts His favour, glory be to Him! He is born and lives on the surface of the earth. He ploughs his furrow in life. He cleaves to it with his will and volition. He strives. He is miserable and tired. He proceeds on his life journey and returns in the end to his Creator who will question him and call him to account. He will reap the fruits of his efforts and toil in this world. He will stay forever either in the bliss of Paradise or the torment of Hellfire. Do not seek rest, happiness, and bliss on the surface of the earth. Project your sight to what is beyond it. Seek those things in the Next World, in the world of eternal timelessness. This world is a mixture of rest and toil, happiness and misery, bliss and hell. True bliss exists only in the Garden.

Live however you wish, you will die in the end. Love whomever you wish, you must part from them. Own whatever you wish, it is but dust. Only your actions will accompany you – your actions which you will find present on the Day of Reckoning. You will find them present in your Book. It is a book with voice, form and movement. O child of Adam, do not be astonished. The crime you committed in secret will take shape before your eyes, testifying against you. You will find the righteous actions you performed in secret present before you, testifying on your behalf. You will see and hear every word and action which came from you, by the permission of Allah.

It will be as if you were watching a film in which you are the protagonist. You will relive your life in this world from your birth to your death. You will live it again in full on the Day of Reckoning with Allah's permission and you will burn with anger and shame or leap with joy. *"... They will find there everything they did and your Lord will not wrong anyone."* (18:49) and *"...Allah has counted it while they have forgotten it. Allah is Witness of all things."* (58:6)

What is this awesome comprehensiveness? What are these books? How can they be recorded when we are asleep and heedless? I confess that I do not know. And you, reader, do not know either. No creature in existence can take anything from Allah's pre-eternal knowledge except what the All-Knowing Giver allows him. Modern human science has managed to record and replay some events from the past. It has achieved a manner of listening to and seeing individuals who are now dead. The limited abilities of man have managed to invent radio and television. How much more extensive is the power of the All-Seeing, All-Hearing, which has no limits! How incomparably great is the power of the Creator and Fashioner!

The books of our actions are not mere books to be read which the angels write with paper and pen. They are not books whose contents any person might deny. They are powerful books acting by themselves as an undeniable proof which does not require any further witness. They are books which are written and inscribed about us by the angels in a form to which we have no access in this life.

When we die, our words and actions remain and do not vanish. They remain suspended in space. Our voices and forms remain after our death as patterns which can be regenerated. Scientific research has established that our voices create waves in the air and those waves continue through the ether. It is the same with any action that we perform, whether in the light or darkness. Heat issues from it and the heat remains suspended in space in the form of waves. Modern science can track the heat waves issuing from any being. Human efforts can pick up events which occurred some hours ago but cannot discern events which occurred a long time

132

ago. If modern human knowledge has been able to achieve this much, imagine what unlimited Divine knowledge is capable of!

> "Say: 'Allah gives you life, then makes you die, and then will gather you together to the Day of Rising of which there is no doubt. Yet most people do not know.' To Allah belongs the sovereignty of the heavens and earth, and on the day that the Hour occurs, that Day the falsifiers will be the losers. You will see every nation on its knees, every nation summoned to its Book: 'Today you shall be repaid for what you did. This is Our Book speaking against you with the truth. We have been recording all that you were doing.'" (45:26-29)

In a *hadith qudsi* reported by Abu Dharr, may Allah be pleased with him, we learn that the Prophet, may Allah bless him and grant him peace, said in what he related from his Lord Almighty: "My slaves, I have forbidden Myself injustice and made it forbidden among you, so do not commit injustice. O My slaves, all of you are astray except those whom I guide, so ask Me for guidance and I will guide you. O My slaves, all of you are hungry except those whom I feed, so ask Me to feed you and I will feed you. O My slaves, all of you are naked except those whom I clothe, so ask me to clothe you and I will clothe you. O My slaves, you commit sins by night and by day and I forgive all sins, so ask My forgiveness and I will forgive you. O My slaves, you will never attain to My power of harming so as to harm Me and you will never attain to My power of benefiting so as to benefit Me. O My slaves, if the first of you and the last of you, men and jinn, had hearts like that of the most godfearing man among you, that would not increase My kingdom in any way. O My slaves, if the first of you and the last of you, men and jinn, had hearts like that of the most profligate among you, that would not decrease My kingdom in any way. O My slaves, if the first of you and the last of you, men and jinn, were to stand all on one plateau and ask of Me, I could give each man what he asked for and it would not diminish what I have any more than a needle put in the sea would diminish it. O My slaves, it is your actions which I reckon for you and then I will requite you for them. Whoever finds good should praise Allah. Whoever finds other than that should blame no one but himself." (Muslim)

The Opening of the Books

"When the written pages are opened up." (81:10)

The Preserved Tablet will be raised and shown to the Assembly and in front of it will emerge a clearly visible line of writing: "There is no god but Allah alone. His *deen* is Islam. Muhammad is His slave and His Messenger. Whosoever believes in Allah and affirms His promise and follows His Messengers, I will admit him to the Garden." (*Misbah as-Sunna,* al-Baghawi)

The mercy of Allah manifests itself before the gathered masses of the human race, since it was written in the Preserved Tablet: "My mercy has precedence over My wrath." Then there is a great shock – a terrible disgrace. The Preserved Tablet proclaims the actions of all creatures, presenting them to everyone simultaneously. They will be displayed to all. The veils will be rent and drop and all secrets will be disclosed. People will be disgraced. All that was concealed in this world will be uncovered. Everything will be laid bare before the huge throngs of Allah's creation in the face of His Majesty.

Every creature will read his actions and the actions of other people. He will read them with mixed feelings and different emotions, contradictory and clashing. He will read them with regret and care, shame and embarrassment, yet with great eagerness. He will see the stories of all of Allah's creatures from the beginning of this world to its end. Important startling secrets will be disclosed to him, whose truth he did not know in this world.

There is intense terror, burning terror. Everyone will stand there divested of all strength and power, divested of everything, including all their contriving and scheming, standing under the throne of the All-Merciful, the Compeller in the midst of the huge crowd without any covering. What an extraordinary book it is! *"A Book*

135

which does not pass over any action, small or great, without recording it." (18:49) The Preserved Tablet means universal disgrace for every proud foul tyrant and noble honour for every striving wronged believer.

The Messengers and Prophets will be questioned. The angels will be questioned. The latter will be questioned but not taken to account. The events of the Day of Rising will continue, until the Call is heard. A immense compelling voice will be heard, a voice resounding from all sides: "O Company of jinn and men! I have listened to you since I created you until this day, hearing your words and seeing your actions. So listen to Me. These are your actions and pages which will be read to you. Anyone who finds good should praise Allah. Anyone who finds other than that, should blame no one but himself." (From a *hadith* in Abu Ya'la)

There will be calls to the different communities. Every nation will be summoned in the name of the Messenger whom they follow, or in the name of the Path by which they were guided, or in the name of any Imam whom they followed in this world. The pages will be opened to every nation, to every single individual among them. *"On the Day We summon all people with their records. Those who are given their book in their right hand will read their book and they will not be wronged by even the tiniest shred. Anyone who is blind in this world will be blind in the Next world and even further off the path."* (17:71-72) *"We have fastened the destiny of every man about his neck and on the Day of Rising We will bring out a book for him which he will find spread open in front of him."* (17:13)

The books will be opened in full view of everyone. People will melt from shame in the midst of the crowd – the throng of men, jinn and angels. They will tremble from the distress of exposure in the midst of that awesome gathering of the creatures of Allah. They will stream with sweat. Yet how ridiculous that is! Who is going to think of anyone other than himself in those terrible moments? It is a time when no one will be able to think of anyone but themselves.

Abu Dawud mentioned that 'A'isha, may Allah be pleased with her, said, "I remembered the Fire and wept. The Messenger of

136

Allah, may Allah bless him and grant him peace, asked, 'Why are you weeping?' I replied, 'I remembered the Fire and so I wept. Will you remember your family on the Day of Rising?' He replied, 'There are three places where no one will remember anyone else: at the Balance, until one knows whether it is light or heavy; when the pages fly, until one knows whether he will receive his book in his right hand or his left hand or behind his back; and at the Sirat when it is placed over Jahannam, until one passes over it."

The states of people will differ when the books appear. Some of them have righteous actions and take their books in their right hands. Some of them have foul actions and receive their books in their left hands. But the most wretched and miserable of Allah's creation at that time take their books in their left hands behind their backs. Abu Bakr Ahmad ibn Thabit al-Khatib reported from Zayd ibn Thabit, may Allah be pleased with him, that the Messenger of Allah, may Allah bless him and grant him peace, said, "The first to be given his book in his right hand among this community will be 'Umar ibn al-Khattab, may Allah be pleased with him. It has rays like those of the sun." He was asked, "Where will Abu Bakr be, Messenger of Allah?" He replied "Far from there! The angels will have brought him near the Garden."

When one of us receives his book, his eyes will alight on the first line: *"Read your book! Today your own self is reckoner enough against you!"* (17:14) People will mumble in whispers and stupefaction: "How can your own self be a reckoner against you? What does this mean? Can a man be his own reckoner? Or is it merely a warning?" The pages of the book will be turned and the answer will present itself. Inside it one will witness the film of his life in full, recorded in sound and vision. He will not be able to deny it. People will ask in faint frightened voices, "What is this book? How can it record everything with this extreme precision? Where were we then?" The evildoers will exclaim with regret and contrition: *"Alas for us! What is this Book which does not pass over any action, small or great, without recording it?"* (18:49)

It is unequivocal proof. The lawful is clear and the unlawful is clear. Man will be divested of all his ruses and contrivances. The ambiguities of this world will leave him. There will no misunder-

137

standings. Everything will become crystal clear in its reality. Each man will be judged according to what he finds. He lived his life in this world and he will find it present before him in the Next World in every detail. That is how man becomes a witness against himself on the Day of Rising, a witness to the truth and justice which cannot be evaded on that Day.

The Mercy of the All-Merciful and All-Compassionate will descend on that agonising Day. A believer will be given his book in his right hand. He will read its pages. His actions will be presented before his eyes. There are his evil deeds and good deeds, many of which he will have forgotten; Allah has registered them all. His evil actions will flash by him and he will blanch, his limbs trembling, his heart quaking, tears gushing, melting out of shame before Allah. He will think that he is destroyed. Then a stupendous surprise! There are saving graces surrounding him. It is mercy, absolute Divine Mercy. The believer will find at the end of his book: "These are your evil deeds and I have forgiven you for them. These are your good deeds which I have multiplied for you."

How is that possible? It is the Door of Repentance which Allah has left wide open for all His servants. The Ever-Forgiving, Ever-Turning has promised those who repent that He will replace the evil deeds they did before repentance with good deeds which will be added to their good deeds. What generosity beyond any conception or imagination! The Ever-Generous Answerer not only expunges the evil deeds of one who repents but also changes them into good deeds and adds them to his good deeds. It is a gift of the All-Merciful which He gives to His pious servants.

At-Tabarani related from the *hadith* of Abu'l-Mughira from Safwan ibn 'Umar from 'Abdu'r-Rahman ibn Jubayr from Abu Farwa that he went to the Messenger of Allah, may Allah bless him and grant him peace, and asked, "What do you think about a man who has committed every sin without omitting any of them at all – is repentance possible for him?" He asked, "Have you become Muslim?" He replied, "Yes." He said, "Then perform good actions and renounce evil actions and Allah will turn them all into good actions for you." He asked, "Even my betrayals and iniquities?" He replied, "Yes." He continued to say "Allah is greater" until he had disappeared. *"Except for those who repent and believe and do right action. Allah will transform the wrong actions of such people into good ones. Allah is Ever-Forgiving, Most Merciful."* (25:70) *"But if anyone repents after his wrongdoing, and puts things to rights, Allah will turn towards him. Allah is Ever-Forgiving, All-Compassionate."* (5:39)

The believer who is given his book in his right hand will not be subjected to any reckoning, nor will anything in it be finely scrutinised. He will be given a very easy reckoning. Then he will be saved and joyfully join his family who preceded him to the Garden. 'A'isha, may Allah be pleased with her, reported that the Messenger of Allah, may Allah bless him and grant him peace, said, "Whoever is subjected to the Reckoning will be punished." She remarked, "Does not Allah Almighty say, *'He will be given an easy reckoning'*? (84:8)" He replied, "That does not refer to the Reckoning but to the Presentation (of the books). Whoever is subjected to the Reckoning on the Day of Rising will be punished." (al-Bukhari, Muslim, at-Tirmidhi and an-Nasa'i)

'A'isha also reported, "I heard the Messenger of Allah, may Allah bless him and grant him peace, say in one of his prayers, 'O Allah, give me an easy reckoning!' When he finished, I asked, 'Messenger of Allah, what is an easy reckoning?' He replied, 'That Allah looks at your book and disregards it. Whoever is subjected to the Reckoning on that day, 'A'isha, will be destroyed." (Ahmad)

According to the *Sahih*, when Ibn 'Umar was asked about salvation he reported, "I heard the Messenger of Allah say, may Allah bless him and grant him peace: 'Allah will draw a person near on the Day of Rising and will inform him of all his wrong actions until he thinks that he is destroyed. Allah Almighty will say, "I concealed them for you in the world and I forgive you for them today." Then he will be given the book of his good actions in his right hand. But as for the unbelievers and hypocrites, the witnesses will declare: *"Those are the ones who lied against their Lord. Yes indeed! Allah's curse is on the wrongdoers."* (11:18)'"

A believer will have a difficult and exacting reckoning but after he has been rescued from that agonising situation he will be filled with joy and brimming over with happiness. He will rush among the assembled throngs with his book in his hand, calling out and shouting with joy in a loud voice. All of Allah's creatures will see him and hear him repeating, *"Here, come and read my Book! I counted on meeting my reckoning!"* Then an angel will call, "This is so-and-so who has received a happiness after which he will never be wretched again."

Tears of joy will flow from his eyes and he will fly – fly across the *Sirat*, along with those of the believers like him who have been given an easy reckoning, and he will join his family who preceded him to the Garden. *"As for him who is given his Book in his right hand, he will say, 'Here, come and read my Book! I counted on meeting my reckoning.' He shall have a very pleasant life in an elevated Garden, its ripe fruit hanging close to hand. 'Eat and drink with relish for the things you did before in days gone by!'"* (69:19-24)

"But as for him who is given his Book in his left hand," (69:25) his heart is devoid of faith in Allah and lacking in mercy to Allah's creation. He was a stubborn tyrant, an arrogant wrongdoer. He was not merciful to the weak and poor. He demolished their houses. He expelled people from their homes. He ruined, he destroyed, he tortured. He produced the horrors of this world and so he is cast into the terrors of the Next World.

The pages of his book will be turned, and suddenly his crimes will be present, testifying against him in full detail. He will tremble and will be beset with awful stupefaction. He will melt with regret and remorse. He will be divested of everything. He will become weak and overpowered. There will be no rescue or flight. He will collapse, sobbing. He will shout and call out, *"If only I had not been given my book and had not known about my reckoning! If only death had really been the end! My wealth has been of no avail to me. My authority has disappeared from me."* (69:25-29)

The final Divine Command will issue with full majesty and force, in all its implacable finality. *"Seize him and truss him up. Then roast him in the Blazing Fire. Then bind him in a chain which is seventy cubits long."* (69:30-32) All existence will quake.

140

Allah's creation will tremble from the terror of the Standing. Events will unravel in dumbfounded and apprehensive silence. The angels will swiftly confine the unbelievers in the blink of an eye and seize them with the force and harshness commensurate to their nature and bind them in chains.

They will cry out: "No! Let me go, *Zabaniyya*! Help me, people! Jinn! Can't you save me! O Lord! There is no refuge except in You! Show me mercy! Save me from this! I repent to You! I believe in You! I testify that there is no god but You alone with no partner! I testify that Muhammad is Your slave and Messenger! Yes! I believe in all Your Prophets and Messengers. You will not find any cause to be angry with me after today ever again! Accept my repentance, O Lord of the Worlds! Accept my repentance!" But...'*Allah only accepts the repentance of people who do evil in ignorance and then repent of doing it very soon. Allah turns towards people such as these. Allah is All-Knowing, All-Wise. There is no repentance for people who persist in doing evil deeds until death shows its face to them and then say, 'Now I repent,' nor for people who die as unbelievers. For them We have prepared a painful punishment.*" (4:17-18)

The command is final. Such repentance is not real: it is coerced. The condemned person is no longer able to commit sins. His repentance is not worth a brass farthing. He will never rectify society or benefit existence, and he himself will not benefit from it. Allah knows full well that if he were to be returned to the world a billion times, he would still commit the same wrong actions and would never give them up.

The angels will fan out between the rows, seizing those impious unbelievers like him. They will drag them off with violence and force, bound in chains. They will truss them up in fetters. What immense terror! What a humiliating fearful position to be in – like a chicken roasted on a spit. In fact it is worse – far worse. The unbelievers will suffer but they will not speak. They will not even be able to whisper. Words of rebuke and blame will be heaped on them – and mockery and derision. It is a physical punishment and a psychological punishment.

"Seize him and drag him bodily to the middle of the Blazing Fire. Then pour the punishment of boiling water on his head. 'Taste! You are the mighty one, the noble one! This is the very thing you used to doubt.'" (44:47-50)

His honour is lost. His respect in the eyes of his sons, parents and servants is lost. His honour in the eyes of his family and friends is lost. He is broken and humbled before all of Allah's creation. An angel will call out in the sight and hearing of all of Allah's creation: "This is So-and-so, the son of So-and-so. He is wretched with such a wretchedness after which he will never be happy again." He will be cast into Hell-fire.

The states of people vary according to their actions. One person will have the pages of his book turned and find his actions clear and evident. When his good actions appear, he will think that he will be saved, but suddenly there will be a sentence at the end of the book: "These good actions are taken from you. These evil actions of yours have been multiplied against you." The colour of his face will change. His face will grow dark, overcome with sorrow, grief and despair. He will ask inside himself with choked rage, in a terrified whisper: "How? How can my good actions turn to nothing when I strove to perform them? Why? Why have my bad actions been multiplied? Where is mercy? Where is justice?"

Mercy does not leave him. Justice does not leave him. The covering is removed and in his new form he sees and recognises what he could not see and recognise in this world. He will touch the outspread shade of mercy and become aware of the Balance of Justice set up in the arena of the Reckoning. Mercy will join him. Justice will join him. They will come to him in the vast expanses of the Almighty and he will recognise the reality, the absolute true reality, divested of all personal prejudice: the good actions of a man which are taken away are in compensation for injustices done to others. The good actions are removed from the page of the wrongdoer and added to the page of the wronged person.

The extent of the deletions and additions will vary according to the degree of injustice committed. Some will lose only a portion of their good actions while others have all their good actions removed and transferred to the page of the wronged person. Some people committed many great injustices, so that not only are all their good actions erased but they also take on some of the evil actions of the people they wronged to add to their own evil deeds. In short, the good actions of the unjust on that Day will become the property of those they wronged.

Beware! Beware of wronging others. You toil, you labour, you exert yourself throughout your life, amassing good deeds with which to meet your Lord. Then they become dust: they are lost in injustice with all its forms, varieties and degrees. Recognise your duties towards others in the same way that you claim your rights. Beware! Beware of what you imagine to be small while it is great in the sight of Allah. Beware of slander and backbiting. Beware of defamation and fault-finding. Beware of usurping the rights of others, whatever they may be. Be careful in all your dealings with Allah's creation. The Ever-Forgiving Creator can forgive all wrong actions but the weak creature is not able to forgive a single one.

"O Man! You are toiling laboriously towards your Lord, and meet Him you will. As for him who is given his book in his right hand, he will be given an easy reckoning and return to his family joyfully. But as for him who is given his book behind his back, he will cry out for destruction but will be roasted in a Searing Blaze. He used to be joyful in his family. He thought that he was never to return. But on the contrary his Lord was always watching him."

(84:6-15)

The People who believe in *Tawhid* will Remain

"Or do they have partners for Allah? Then let them produce their partners if they speak the truth! The Day that legs are bared and they are called on to prostrate, but they will not be able to do it. Their eyes will be downcast, darkened by debasement; for they were called on to prostrate when they were in full possession of their faculties." **(68:41-43)**

The Messenger of Allah, may Allah bless him and grant him peace, said, "When Allah gathers the first and the last on the Day of Rising, for a Day of which there is no doubt, a caller will call: 'Whoever did an action for other than Allah, let him seek his reward from other than Allah. Allah is the One who can most dispense with partners." (Ibn Majah; from Abu Sa'd ibn Abi Fadala)

As we have seen, all Allah's creatures will meet on the Day of Meeting. They will meet and then be divided up into believers, hypocrites, idolaters and unbelievers. The last three groups will be dealt with and taken to the Fire and only the those who affirmed Allah's Unity will remain: those who said: "There is no god but Allah." All who said that remain, whether they acted on it or not. There are some of them who obeyed Allah and followed His path, some who disobeyed and did not follow His Path, some who committed minor wrong actions, and some who committed major wrong actions.

Some of them will enter Paradise after the Reckoning and some of them will be punished in the Fire according to their wrong actions after a difficult reckoning, until the mercy of Allah reaches

144

them and brings them into the Garden. In other words, none of these people will be in the Fire forever. In the end, they will all reach the Garden. One thing unites them: belief in the Oneness of Allah – glory be to Him and may He be exalted! They will be gathered together. They will be gathered and will witness the terrors of the Day of Distinguishing.

"Allah does not forgive partners being attributed to Him but He forgives anything besides that to anyone He wills. He who attributes partners to Allah is greatly misguided." (4:116) So the idolaters are led off in groups to be cast, along with their deities, into the flames of Hellfire. There are cries of woe and punishment, reverberating echoes of shouts throughout the place. There will be terrible fear and alarm, terrible constriction and grief. Only the affirmers of Divine Unity are left waiting, alert, longing for the moment when that terrible arduous standing will end. It is a great test, a hard, arduous trial.

Finally the light of guidance will burst forth, illuminating the hearts of the believers. At last the All-Holy King will be manifested to the believers. Tranquillity will descend into their hearts and they will recognise Him immediately. Recognition of Allah does not depend on the eyes. It has no need of tangible material evidence. The Almighty All-High will manifest Himself, even if it be from a distance or from behind a veil. He will manifest Himself in a manner which only He knows and which will touch the core of the heart, the spirit. Then people's souls will be filled with longing and their eyes will overflow with tears – tears of awe and humility. The believers will fall down in prostration to Allah, the Lord of the Worlds.

Mu'adh ibn Jabal reported that the Messenger of Allah, may Allah bless him and grant him peace, stated, "If you like, I will tell you the first thing which Allah Almighty will say to the believers on the Day of Resurrection and the first thing that they will say to Him." They replied, "Please do, Messenger of Allah!" He said, "Allah Almighty will ask the believers, 'Did you desire to meet Me?' They will reply, 'Yes, O Lord!' He will continue, 'What made that so?' They will reply, 'Your pardon, mercy and pleasure.' He will say, 'I have made My mercy mandatory for you.'"

The disobedient will remain with their covering removed. Their real nature will be disclosed to the assembly. People who committed grave wrong actions and those who did not pray or prostrate to Allah when they were able to do so will be among them. They will be summoned to prostrate on that day but will not be able to. Their backs will have become like wooden planks. Whenever they try to prostrate, they will fall backwards. They will be like boards which cannot bend or fold. The events on the Day of Recompense will proceed inexorably. The Decisive Moment, the moment of Reckoning, will have arrived.

> "Whether We show you something of what We have promised them or We take you back to Us, conveying the Message is your responsibility and the Reckoning is Ours. Do they not see how We come to the land, eroding it from its extremities? Allah judges and there is no reversing His judgement. He is Swift at Reckoning." (13:40-41)

Entering the Garden without Reckoning

"And those who were fearful of their Lord
will be driven to the Garden in companies..."
(39:73)

The process will unfold step by implacable step. The Fire will be looking on fixedly, black and dark, erupting and boiling, its sound reverberating. The *Sirat* will be suspended above it: a bridge which is narrower than the blade of the sharpest sword, thinner than the finest hair. Woe betide anyone who is compelled to cross it with his back weighed down by sins and wrong actions! The Garden lies beyond the *Sirat*, to the right of the Throne. It will appear very very far away but it will be indescribably beautiful – resplendent, shining and radiant, lofty, splendid and peerless!

The Messengers and Prophets will cross over. They will cross the *Sirat* while the Fire below is quiescent. Its sound and flames will abate. Its darkness will disperse and the light of the Prophets, peace and blessings be upon them, will radiate. A light will issue forth, flowing from their incomparably fine and sublime qualities; a light which will fill the horizons, spreading in every direction. The Prophets will cross over the *Sirat* swifter than a flash and enter the Garden. The first of them to enter it will be Muhammad, may Allah bless him and grant him peace.

Muslim reported from Anas ibn Malik that the Messenger of Allah, may Allah bless him and grant him peace, said, "I will have the most followers on the Day of Rising and I will be the first to knock on the gate of the Garden."

The command of Allah will issue forth, the voice of the Guide, the Light, calling out, "Where are Muhammad and his Community! Muhammad! Admit to the Garden those of your Community who owe no reckoning or punishment!"

147

The Nation of Muhammad will come in succession, group after group, led by the Prophet, may Allah bless him and grant him peace, into the Garden. He will lead them holding in his hand the Banner of Praise, on which will be written: "There is no god but Allah. Muhammad is the Messenger of Allah."

Ibrahim's Community will follow, led into the Garden by him, peace be upon him. All the Communities will pass over the *Sirat* one after another on the heels of their noble Prophets. Those who will enter the Garden without Reckoning are the true, the martyrs, the people of knowledge and the believers who were steadfast, full of praise of their Lord, and who relied on Allah as He should be relied upon. Such people will enter the Garden without reckoning, but on one condition – on condition that they no injustice outstanding towards any creature at all.

Then an immense blackness will fill the horizon – an awesome mass of people, their faces shining like the full moon. Yes, they are the community of Muhammad, the first Community to cross the *Sirat* and enter the Garden, greater than any of the other Communities in number. At the front of them will be Abu Bakr as-Siddiq. Their light will go before them. Radiant light will spread from their faces. They will form an awesome procession and a matching procession of angels will meet them with honour, respect and greeting. They will enter the Garden throng upon throng.

Then a lone voice will echo across the horizons, a tender heart-rending voice, a strong voice, crying, "One! One! One! One!" The resonance of these words will penetrate everyone's hearts and ears and all will be moved. Those crossing the *Sirat* will hesitate and the rest of the people will hesitate behind them: "One! One! One! One!" Tears will flow, tears of awe and humility, tears of belief and certainty, tears of joy in that Immense Station. Then the same voice will call, and all the people behind him will call out: "Allah is Greater! Allah is Greater! I testify that there is no God but Allah. I testify that Muhammad is the Messenger of Allah."

Yes, it is Bilal ibn Rabah, the first *mu'adhdhin* of Islam, the *mu'adhdhin* of the Messenger of Allah, peace and blessings be upon him. It is Bilal, the black Abyssinian slave. Despite the blackness of his skin, he will shine with light and radiance. He will radiate a glow on that immense day. He is the poor weak slave, the slave whose abilities were released by Islam which liberated him and made him one of the greatest men the world has known. Bilal was the man who endured the most severe and harshest forms of torture. He bore them with complete constancy, strength, resolve and determination. He began to repeat his eternal refrain, the refrain which has come down through the passage of time, "One! One! One! One!" until Abu Bakr as-Siddiq bought him and set him free. He is the man about whom 'Umar ibn al-Khattab said, "Abu Bakr is our master and he set free our master." The report of Muhammad, peace and blessings be upon him, is realised: Muhammad, who always said that Bilal was a man of the Garden.

Here are the martyrs of Islam: Here is Sumayya, the first martyr in Islam from the Community of Muhammad. Here is Yasir. Here is 'Ammar ibn Yasir. They will shine on the *Sirat*. Their faces will sparkle with light as they cross the *Sirat* with complete firmness and gravity. A halo of honour and nobility will surround them. The angels will greet them warmly. They endured various forms of torture, abasement and humiliation. They were steadfast and hoped for the highest reward: Sumayya, the mother of 'Ammar, was killed under torture by Abu Jahl. 'Ammar's father Yasir also died from the severe torture. 'Ammar passed through many tribulations and was finally martyred at the Battle of Siffin at the age of seventy.

The Messenger of Allah, may Allah bless him and grant him peace, used to go to Yasir's family when they were being tortured. He tried to alleviate their burden. He revived their heroism and courage and made them firm in belief. His tender heart wept for them out of compassion and mercy at the torture which they were receiving which was beyond the capacity of any human being to bear, so that one day 'Ammar was forced to call out to the Messenger of Allah saying, "Messenger of Allah, we cannot bear it any more!" The Messenger, peace and blessing be upon him, called, "Fortitude, family of Yasir! You are promised the Garden!"

The delegations will continue to arrive at the Garden from all Communities. The martyr of Islam in the time of Musa, peace be upon him, will appear – the great woman whose name is joined in the Qur'an with the name of Maryam, daughter of 'Imran, which gives her a high position among the women of all time.

> *"Allah has coined a likeness for those who believe: the wife of Pharaoh when she said, 'My Lord, build a house in the Garden for me in Your Presence, and rescue me from Pharaoh and all his deeds, and rescue me from the wrong-doing people.' And Maryam, daughter of 'Imran, who guarded her chastity, and We breathed Our Spirit into her; and she confirmed the words of her Lord and His Book, and was one of the obedient."* (66:11-12)

The wife of Pharaoh was a believer: Asiya bint Muzaham, may Allah be pleased with her, believed in the message of Musa, peace be upon him. She said, "I believe in the Lord of Musa and Harun. I believe in Allah, the One, the Unique." When Pharaoh learned of that, he inflicted on her the harshest and most severe torture but she turned to her Lord, calling out with belief and firm certitude: *"My Lord, build a house in the Garden for me in Your Presence."* She looked towards heaven, looking at her house in the Garden and smiled. Pharaoh was dumbfounded. He said, "I inflict this on her and she laughs!" Then he commanded his aides to bring a huge stone and he said, "If she continues in her heresy drop it on top of her. If she retracts, she is my wife." Asiya remained firm in her belief and her soul ascended to her Creator. The stone was dropped onto her lifeless body. On the Day of Rising her soul will return to her body so that she may receive the promise of her Lord and obtain her house in the Garden.

I am tired of having to speak about the injustice of man towards his fellow man. I detest the cruelty and brutality of man to man, acts which turn into mere words that are written and lines that are read. These words can do very little to convey the reality of the great terrors that human beings endure, terrors which only a very few can remain firm in the face of, terrors which have plagued humanity throughout the course of its history.

Will there be nothing but horror on the Day of Rising? There is no denying that the Day of Rising holds immense terrors, terrors such as no creature can imagine; but they will only befall those who fashioned them with their own hands in this world – like Iblis, Pharaoh, Nimrod, Abu Jahl, Abu Lahab, and other shaytans of men and jinn who have spread throughout the ages in various parts of the world. Such people deserve only to be cast into Jahannam without reckoning.

However, let us return to the *Sirat* and those who enter the Garden without reckoning. A call will go out for the blind, those who were deprived of the blessing of sight in this world but did not complain; people who did not doubt and did not ever despair of the mercy of Allah, who did not forget all the blessings of Allah to them which cannot be counted or numbered. They were adorned with steadfastness and pleasure, thankfulness and praise, trust in Allah and continuing in action and constant striving throughout their lives. Such people will cross the *Sirat* with their eyesight restored to them. A banner will be raised for them in the hand of Shu'ayb, peace be upon him, who will lead them into the Garden.

Another call will go out for those who suffered trials and afflictions. A banner will be raised for them by the hand of Ayyub, peace be upon him: Ayyub, who was steadfast in illness, poverty and loss of family and friends. He did not despair of the mercy of Allah. He did not despair or give up. He was constant in worship, thankfulness, praise, and reliance on his Almighty Lord.

A call will go out for the people of chastity and purity, young men and women to whom the doors of marriage were closed and to whom the doors of the unlawful were wide open, but who nonetheless remained chaste and steadfast and did not go near fornication. A banner will be raised for them by the hand of Yusuf, peace be upon him, and they will enter the Garden.

A call will go out for the wealthy who were godfearing. A banner will be raised for them by the hand of Sulayman, peace be upon him: Sulayman, to whom Allah gave prophethood, wealth, rank, and power. He gave him a kingdom greater than He gave to anyone else on earth – a kingdom which included power over human beings, jinn, birds, and the wind. Despite that, Sulayman applied himself to worship, praised Allah, and was steadfast. He was steadfast in the face of all those temptations, enticements and responsibilities and was not arrogant for an instant. He did not take advantage of his wealth or use it in any manner not pleasing to Allah. He spent it only in the Way of Allah. His kingdom did not distract him from worshipping Allah as He should be worshipped, and he judged with nothing but justice.

Those delegations will hasten on, their light running with them on the *Sirat*. Angels will escort them to the Garden. Shouts of glorification and praise will rise up, proclaiming Allah One and declaring Him great.

The tears of the believers who have not yet crossed the *Sirat* will flow copiously, believers of every community who still await the appointed Reckoning. A believer among them will pause, forgetting the terror of the Standing where he is. He will gaze at the horizon, contemplating that wonderful sight. His entire being will shake with amazement and astonishment. He will tremble with joy. How often he heard or read about the Messengers and Prophets of Allah! He believed in all of them, peace and blessings be upon them. He was contemporary with one of them in this world, but not with all of them. Now at the end of time he will see them all with his own eyes. They will pass across the *Sirat* in majesty and gravity. Their light will radiate and shine in the Next World as it shone in this world.

There is the Beloved of Allah, Muhammad. He has crossed the *Sirat* and the gates of the Garden have been opened for him. He has entered it. There are the Friend of Allah, Ibrahim; the Spirit of Allah, 'Isa; the one to whom He spoke, Musa; His chosen one Adam; and His grateful servant Nuh. There are Isma'il, Ishaq, Ya'qub, Yunus, Yusuf, Da'ud, Sulayman and the rest of the Prophets of Allah Almighty. Behind them are the true and the people of knowledge, the martyrs and the righteous friends of Allah who will enter the Garden without reckoning.

The heart of the believer will flutter at that majestic spectacle. His heart will swell with joy. He will weep tears of awe, exaltation and esteem. He will weep with the sweetest and most beautiful weeping in existence. His yearning will be intense. He will wish that he could stretch out his hand to a Prophet and clasp it, to address him, to befriend him. But his time has not yet come.

152

Steadfastness and the Path to the Garden

The steadfast who enter the Garden without reckoning are numerous; but they are very few when compared with the rest of Allah's creation, a few existing in various areas of the earth throughout the whole extent of time. There are those who were killed in the ruinous wars between believers and unbelievers over the course of history - victims who were steadfast and expected their reward with firm belief and utter certainty. There are the victims mentioned in history and the victims known only to the All-Hearing, All-Seeing.

Steadfastness, however, does not consist only of fortitude in the face of the suffering of wars alone. Indeed, steadfastness takes many forms. You yourself may be one of those steadfast ones who will enter the Garden without reckoning. Who knows? Your family or friends or neighbours may take refuge in you to intercede for them with the Lord of the Worlds. Those are matters of which no one can have sure knowledge and which no one knows except Allah Almighty.

In one *hadith* from 'A'isha, may Allah be pleased with her, we find that the Messenger of Allah, may Allah bless him and grant him peace, said: "O 'A'isha, this world is not appropriate for Muhammad or the family of Muhammad. O 'A'isha! Allah Almighty is only pleased for the people of resolve among the Prophets to be steadfast in the face of what is disagreeable and in the face of what is agreeable. Then He is only pleased to charge me with the same as He charged them with. He said, *'Therefore be steadfast, as those of the Messengers with firm resolve also showed steadfastness.'* (46:35). By Allah, I will do all that I can do to be as steadfast as they were, but there is no strength except by Allah."[1]

---

1. Transmitted by Ibn Abi Hatim. The Messengers with 'firm resolve' were Nuh, Ibrahim, Musa, 'Isa and Muhammad.

Al-Bukhari related that Anas, may Allah be pleased with him, said that he heard the Messenger of Allah say, may Allah bless him and grant him peace: "Allah Almighty has said, 'If I test My slave regarding the two things he loves and he shows fortitude, I will repay him for them with the Garden.'" He meant his eyes.

Al-Bukhari also related from Abu Hurayra, may Allah be pleased with him, reported that the Messenger of Allah said, may Allah bless him and grant him peace: "Allah Almighty says, 'The Garden is the reward for My believing slave when I take back those who are dearest to him of the people of this world and he hopes to be rewarded for it only with the Garden.'"

Abu Ayyub al-Ansari, may Allah be pleased with him, reported that the Messenger of Allah, may Allah bless him and grant him peace said: "There is one statement the learning of which is better for a believer than worshipping for a year and freeing one of the descendants of Isma'il: those who seek Allah, women who obey their husbands, and children who are dutiful to their parents will all enter the Garden without reckoning." (al-Qurtubi)

Ibn Mas'ud said, "Any believer who digs a well in a wilderness in expectation of the reward will enter the Garden without reckoning."

Muslim related from Abu Hurayra, may Allah be pleased with him, that the Messenger of Allah said, may Allah bless him and grant him peace: "By the One Who has my soul in His Hand, you will not enter the Garden until you believe; and you will not believe until you love one another. Shall I direct you to something to do which will give you love of one another? Make the greeting common practice among you."

The Prophet, may Allah bless him and grant him peace, said, "When a man loves his brother, he should tell him that he loves him." (at-Tirmidhi, from al-Miqdad)

Muslim related from Abu Hurayra that the Messenger of Allah said, may Allah bless him and grant him peace: "Allah Almighty will say on the Day of Rising, 'Where are those who loved one another for the sake of My Majesty? Today, on the day when there is no shade but My shade, I will shade them.'"

Anas, may Allah be pleased with him, reported that the Messenger of Allah said, may Allah bless him and grant him peace: "When Allah desires good for one of His slaves, He brings forward the punishment for him in this world. When Allah desires ill for His slave, He withholds from him what is due to him on account of his wrong actions and then settles it on the Day of Rising." The Prophet, may Allah bless him and grant him peace, said, "The greatest reward goes together with the greatest affliction. When Allah Almighty loves people, He tests them. All who are content receive His good pleasure. Those who are angry incur His anger." (at-Tirmidhi)

Abu Hurayra, may Allah be pleased with him, reported that the Messenger of Allah said, may Allah bless him and grant him peace: "Believers, both men and women, will continue to be afflicted in respect of themselves, their children, and their property, until they meet Allah without any wrong actions at all (to account for)." (at-Tirmidhi)

The Messenger of Allah, may Allah bless him and grant him peace, said, "What an extraordinary thing the business of the believer is! All of it is good for him – and that only applies to the believer. If good fortune is his lot, he is grateful and it is good for him. If something harmful happens to him, he is steadfast and that too is good for him too." (Muslim, from Suhayb ibn Sinan)

The Messenger of Allah, may Allah bless him and grant him peace, observed: "On the Day of Rising, four will enter the Garden without reckoning: a scholar who acted on his knowledge, someone who went on *hajj* and then did not behave lewdly or iniquitously for the rest of his life, a martyr killed in battle to establish Islam, and a generous man who earned money by lawful means and then spent it in the Way of Allah without showing off. Those will vie with one another to see which will enter the Garden first."

Ibn 'Abbas reported that the Messenger of Allah said, may Allah bless him and grant him peace: "Allah has slaves whom He has singled out with blessings for the benefit of other people. Whoever is miserly with those blessings, Allah will remove them from him and transfer them to someone else."

The Prophet, may Allah bless him and grant him peace, said: "Generosity is one of the trees of the Garden whose branches extend down to earth. Whoever takes one of its branches, that branch will lead him to the Garden."

Jabir, may Allah be pleased with him, said that the Prophet was asked, "Messenger of Allah, what is the best action?" He replied, "Steadfastness and magnanimity."

Al-Miqdam ibn Shurayh reported that his grandfather said, "Messenger of Allah, direct me to an action which will enable me to enter the Garden." He replied, "Among the things which bring about forgiveness are giving food, extending the greeting, and speaking good words."

The Prophet said, may Allah bless him and grant him peace: "Allah has made the Garden mandatory for anyone who gives shelter to an orphan and feeds him."

The Prophet, may Allah bless him and grant him peace, said, "When an orphan is beaten, the Throne of the All-Merciful is shaken by his weeping. Allah Almighty asks: 'O My angels! Who is making this child weep whose father has vanished into the earth?'"

Al-Bukhari related from Sahl ibn Sa'd, may Allah be pleased with him, that the Messenger of Allah stated, may Allah bless him and grant him peace: "I and those who care for orphans shall be in the Garden like this," and he pointed with his forefinger and middle finger and made an opening between them.

The Messenger of Allah, may Allah bless him and grant him peace, said, "I will be the first for whom the gate of the Garden will open; but I will see a woman coming towards me and I will ask, 'What is it and who are you?" She will say, "I am a widow who stayed with her orphaned children." (Abu Ya'la)

Muslim report that 'A'isha recounted, may Allah be pleased with her: "A poor woman came to me with her two daughters and I gave her three dates. She gave one to each of them and lifted the third to her mouth to eat it. Then her daughters asked for it and she divided between them the date she had intended to eat. I was astonished at this and mentioned it to the Messenger of Allah, may Allah bless him and grant him peace. He said, 'Allah has made the

Garden mandatory for her on account of it and freed her from the Fire.'"

There are many *hadiths* of the Messenger of Allah, may Allah bless him and grant him peace, on this subject. One of them is from Ibn Majah: "The best of houses among the Muslims is a house which contains an orphan who is treated well, and the worst house among the Muslims is a house which contains an orphan who is treated badly."

As Ibn Majah also related, "He who strives on behalf of a widow and the very poor is like one who fights for the Cause of Allah or who stands in prayer at night and fasts during the day."

The Prophet, may Allah bless him and grant him peace, said. "O Allah, I am the one who most takes care of the rights of the weak, orphans and women." (an-Nasa'i)

Abu'd-Darda' 'Umaymir, may Allah be pleased with him, said that he heard the Messenger of Allah say, may Allah bless him and grant him peace: "Help me in seeking out the weak: they must be supported. You are only provided for on account of the weak among you." (Abu Dawud)

Here is a story about honouring widows and orphans. It took place long ago but has been repeated many times. Once there was a family in affluent circumstances. Then their provider died and his wife and daughters were bereaved: their circumstances changed and they became so poor that they left their homeland fearing abuse. They reached a town and entered a mosque. The mother left her daughters there and went out to look for food. She passed by an important man of the town who was a Muslim and explained her situation, but he did not believe her.

"You must bring me proof," he said.

"I am a stranger," she replied.

So he turned away from her.

Then she passed by a Magian and told him her story. His heart went out to her and he believed her. He sent one of his wives to her, and she went and brought the woman and her children to her house and honoured them.

That night the Muslim dreamed that it was the Day of Rising and that the Prophet, may Allah bless him and grant him peace, was there with the Banner of Praise above his head; and beside him there was a huge palace.

"Messenger of Allah, for whom is this palace?" he asked.

"A Muslim man," he replied.

"I am a Muslim," the man said.

"Bring me proof," said the Prophet, may Allah bless him and grant him peace.

The man was shocked. The Prophet, may Allah bless him and grant him peace, reminded him of the widow and the man realised and deeply regretted having turned her away When he woke up he went to look for her and found out that she was in the house of the Magian. He went to him and asked for her, but the Magian refused and said, "We have received much blessing from them."

"Take a thousand dinars and let me have them," said the Muslim.

The Magian refused and said, "The palace you dreamed of was created for me. Do you boast of your Islam to me? By Allah, neither I nor my family went to sleep before we had become Muslim at the hand of that widow. Then I had the same dream as you. The Messenger of Allah, may Allah bless him and grant him peace, asked me, 'Are the widow and her daughters with you?' I replied, 'Yes, Messenger of Allah.' He said, 'The palace is for you and your family.'"

Only Allah can gauge the remorse, grief and regret which that Muslim felt.

Imam Ahmad ibn Hanbal relates something from 'Abdullah ibn 'Amr ibn al-'As, may Allah be pleased with him, about honouring the poor Muhajirun who feared Allah and relied on Him and were steadfast in poverty, exile and humiliation, seeking the pleasure of their Lord. He reports that the Messenger of Allah, may Allah bless him and grant him peace, said, "Do you know who among Allah's creation will enter the Garden first?"

They said, "Allah and His Messenger know best."

"The first of Allah's creation to enter the Garden will be the poor Muhajirun who defended the Muslims' weak frontiers and protected them from disliked things. Some of them died with what they needed in front of them but lacking the means to acquire it. Allah Almighty will say to those angels He wishes: 'Come here and greet them.' The angels will say, 'We live in Your Heaven and are the best of Your creation. Do You command us to go to those and greet them?' He will say, 'They were slaves who worshipped Me and did not attribute partners to Me. They guarded the weak frontiers and protected people against disliked things and some of them died with what they needed in front of them but lacking the means to acquire it.'" He said, "Then the angels will go to them and enter to them from every door, saying, *'Peace be upon you because of your steadfastness! How wonderful is the Ultimate Abode!'*" (15:24)

Al-Husayn ibn 'Ali, may Allah be pleased with them both, said: "My grandfather, may Allah bless him and grant him peace – told me, 'O my son, you must be content and then you will be independent of people. You must perform the obligations, and then you will be the most devout of people. My son, there is a tree in Paradise called the Tree of Affliction which will be given on the Day of Rising to the people who suffered affliction. No balance will be set up for them, nor will any register be unrolled for them. Their reward will be poured out on them.' Then he recited, may Allah bless him and grant him peace: *"The steadfast shall be paid their reward in full without any reckoning."* (39:10)

The core of this statement is the reference to those who will enter the Garden without reckoning. Not all people of knowledge and martyrs will enter the Garden before the Reckoning, nor will all those who loved one another for the sake of Allah. Not all those who lost their sight or whose children died will enter the Garden without Reckoning, nor will every son who was dutiful to his parents or every woman who was obedient to her husband. Those and others will not enter the Garden without Reckoning unless they possess the other attributes of those who will enter the Garden without Reckoning.

Those who will enter the Garden without reckoning are the believers who are steadfast and praiseworthy and who do not pay attention to omens or portents but rely on their Lord. Reliance on

159

Allah does not mean incapacity arising from cowardice and laziness, nor does it mean weakness and neglect of rights. It means striving and defending the Truth, exertion and constant action to please Allah. Reliance on Allah is fear of Allah and strength. It is firm belief in the Decree and Decision of Allah. It is utter certainty in the power of Allah Almighty which has no limits.

If something that a believer wants is not achieved after he has undertaken the necessary means, he is patient. He is satisfied with what Allah has prescribed for him. He says with complete certainty that Allah Almighty alone is the One Who has the power to remove harm from him. He says, with a heart at peace: "Allah is enough for me and the best Guardian. We belong to Allah and to Him we return."

That is the proper way to use these phrases, and it brings a result whose end is guaranteed, as happened with Ibrahim, the father of the Prophets, peace and blessings be upon him. He used all possible means to call his people to the truth and did not hesitate for an instant or weaken in the face of Nimrod's tyrannical might. When all means of resistance were exhausted and Ibrahim's enemy overcame him and threw him into the fire he had no power nor strength against it, since there is no power nor strength except by Allah, the All-High, the Immense. But Ibrahim was satisfied with the decree and decision of Allah. He said with a heart at peace and confident in the power of Allah, "Allah is enough for me and the best Guardian." That is the right way to use the phrase. Allah was enough for him and averted harm from him. He commanded the fire to be coolness and peace for Ibrahim and it did not harm him at all.

Reliance on Allah does not means throwing oneself into destruction. It means taking precautions and using means with intelligence and wisdom. Abu Ibrahim 'Abdullah ibn Abi Awfa, may Allah be pleased with him, reported that during one of the battles in which the Messenger of Allah, may Allah bless him and grant him peace, met the enemy, he waited until the sun declined and then stood up to address the people and said: "O people! Do not be too eager to meet the enemy. Ask Allah for well-being. When you do meet them, be steadfast and know that Paradise lies in the shadow of the swords." Then the Prophet said, may Allah bless him and grant him peace: "O Allah, Revealer of the Book and Mover of the clouds and Vanquisher of the Companies, defeat them and help us against them!" (Agreed upon)

Reliance on Allah means recognising Allah as He should be recognised and having utter certainty in His power which knows no limits. It is complete trust and firm belief that His determination and decree is good in its reality, even if it seems outwardly evil. Reliance on Allah means entrusting matters to Him alone and having a good opinion of Him while utilising all necessary means, and then submitting to His decision and decree and being satisfied with His judgement.

The story of the mother of Musa, peace be upon him, provides us with a very good example of reliance on Allah. When Pharaoh was tyrannical and ordered the male children of the Tribe of Israel to be killed at birth, she had no means to save her son and stopped in confusion, unable to protect him, nevertheless, she did not submit to the command of the tyrannical despot. Allah inspired her to suckle her child and then cast him into the river, and Musa's mother did so. She did not did find any security for her baby while he was in her arms and under her eyes; she cast him into the waves under the protection of Allah Almighty.

She utilised the available means and suckled him and placed him in a box. She entrusted her care to Allah with complete trust and certitude. Then she cast her child into the river with a tranquil heart and firm faith. And she did not cease her efforts at that point. She continued to make use of means, and she sent Musa's sister to look for news of him; and events so transpired that her child was returned to her so that she could embrace him, be tender to him and suckle him.

> "We revealed to Musa's mother: 'Nurse him and then, when you fear for him, cast him into the sea. Do not fear or be sad: We shall give him back to you and appoint him to be one of the Messengers.'" (28:7)

Reliance on Allah gives guaranteed strength to him who practises it – strength in both this world and the Next.

"Whoever fears Allah, He will give him a way out and provide for him from somewhere he does not expect. Whoever puts his trust in Allah, He is enough for him. Allah inevitably achieves His aim. Allah has appointed a measure for all things." (65:2-3)

"We shall test you with a certain amount of fear and hunger and loss of wealth and lives and fruits. But give good news to the steadfast: those who, when disaster strikes them, say, 'We belong to Allah and we return to Him.' They are the people who have blessings and mercy from their Lord. It is they who are the guided." (2:155-157)

There is another basic condition for those who enter the Garden without reckoning, which is that they did not commit any act of injustice against any other slave of Allah – they did not wrong a creature either by attitude, word or any other means. That is not the only requirement: there must be no outstanding dispute between the one who enters the Garden without reckoning and his brother, even if he is the one wronged.

Muslim reported from Abu Hurayra, may Allah be pleased with him, that the Messenger of Allah, may Allah bless him and grant him peace, said, "The gates of the Garden are opened on Mondays and Thursdays, and everyone who does not associate anything else with Allah is forgiven except for a man between whom and his brother there is rancour. It is said, 'Wait until these two make it up! Wait until these two make it up!'"

Al-Bukhari reported from Abu Ayyub, may Allah be pleased with him, that the Messenger of Allah said, may Allah bless him and grant him peace: "It is not lawful for a man to dissociate himself from his brother for more than three days so that when they meet, this one turns aside and that one turns aside. The best of them is the one who initiates the greeting."

All who enter the Garden without reckoning will be translucent, their souls pure and at peace, bearing no malice against anyone at all. No one will enter the Garden without reckoning except those purified of their sins and wrong actions before the

Reckoning takes place. There is no one, whether human or jinn, who has no wrong actions, even minor ones, recorded against him. Steadfastness in affliction in its various forms in this world purifies a person of his sins or raises his degrees to that high position until he merits admittance to the Garden without reckoning.

> "...The steadfast shall be paid their wages in full without any reckoning." (39:10)

> "We shall test you until We know the true fighters among you and those who are steadfast, and We test what is reported of you." (47:31)

> "But those who are steadfast and grant forgiveness, that truly shows a firm resolve." (42:43)

People with all these praiseworthy qualities are very rare, and yet they do exist.

As we have seen, it is possible for believers to enter the Garden without any reckoning, or else they might enter it with a light reckoning or after a hard reckoning. It depends on their degree of faith. Rebels and people with major sins among the believers who have not yet been purified of their sins will first enter the Fire, after a difficult reckoning, until they are purified of the impurity of their sins. Then they will enter the Garden.

So it is not simply a case of believers and unbelievers: belief has degrees and disbelief has degrees. Similarly the reward has degrees and the punishment has degrees. The Most Beautiful Names of Allah include: the All-Merciful, the Ever-Merciful, the Just Judge, the Vanquishing Compeller, may He be glorified and hallowed be His Names!

> "In the Name of Allah, All-Merciful, Most Merciful. Praise belongs to Allah, Lord of all the worlds, All Merciful, Most-Merciful, Master of the Day of Repayment." (1:1-4)

Entering the Fire without Reckoning

"The day they are shoved roughly into the Fire of Jahannam: 'This is the Fire you used to deny! Is this then magic? Or it is you that do not see? Roast in it! And bear it patiently - or do not bear it patiently: it makes no difference. You are merely being repaid for what you did.'" (52:13-16)

Pitch-black darkness will prevail and dense smoke will billow up, scorching everything it touches, melting life into the Blazing Fire. Fearful frightened voices will be heard. The seething of Jahannam will increase. It will rise and erupt, seethe and boil. Its rage will intensify: it will fume with wrath through the anger of its Almighty Lord. It will continue in a state of readiness and preparation. It will be prepared and threatening.

The command of Allah will be given. He will call to Adam: "Adam! out of every thousand of your descendants I will put nine hundred and ninety-nine in the Fire and one in the Garden." Distress and terror will prevail. Wits will be lost. Hearts will be in mouths. Limbs will tremble. Feet will shake. Every man and jinn will believe that there is no way he can escape perdition, yet Allah's justice – or rather the mercy of the Almighty – does not demand that.

A black column will emerge from the Fire and swoop towards the evil-doing wrongdoers, towards the people of deviance and misguidance. It will swoop towards them blazing and say, "You trusted three kinds of people: those who claimed there was another god besides Allah; those who did not believe in the Day of Reckoning; and any obdurate tyrant.

*"But instead they deny the Hour; and We have prepared
a Searing Blaze for those who deny the Hour. When it sees
them coming from a long way off, they will hear it
seething and rasping."* (25:11-12)

The angels will spread out carrying chains and shackles, speeding towards the unbelievers, towards Iblis, Yajuj and Majuj and their likes among the shaytans of men and jinn, such as tyrants who had no good actions in their lives. They will try to flee. Their feet will fail them. Their limbs will fail them. The angels will meet them roughly, with harshness and severity appropriate to their nature. The angels will chain their hands and necks to their feet with shackles and fetters.

*"The evildoers will be recognised by their marks and
seized hold of by their forelocks and their feet. Which of
your Lord's blessings do the two of you then deny? This is
Jahannam which the evil-doers deny. They will go to and
fro between fire and scalding water. Which of your Lord's
blessings do the two of you then deny?"* (55:41-45)

A black column of the Fire will swoop down on them, branching out. It will encompass them on all sides. It will gather them up as birds peck up seeds: it will pick them up and drop them into the Fire. People will be out of their minds with terror. Bodies will shake. Shouts for help will be heard. People will call out: "Woe and destruction!" There will be no one to hear or answer them. The Fire of Jahannam will swallow them up. A call will be go up: "Misery with no happiness after it ever!"

*"When they are flung into a narrow place in it, shackled
together in chains, they will cry out there for destruction.
'Do not cry out today for just one destruction: cry out for
many destructions!'"* (25:13-14)

Imam Ahmad ibn Hanbal relates from Anas ibn Malik that the Messenger of Allah, may Allah bless him and grant him peace,

165

said, "The first to be clad in a robe of the Fire will be Iblis. He will place it on his henchmen and drag it from behind and his descendants after him. He will be crying out, 'O for a destruction from which there is no return!' There will be cries of 'O for a destruction from which there is no return!' until they stand at the Fire and he says, 'O for a destruction from which there is no return!' They will be spoken to and will say, 'O for destruction!' *Do not cry out today for just one destruction: cry out for many destructions!*"

The Messenger of Allah, may Allah bless him and grant him peace, said: "Allah will say on the Day of Rising, 'Adam, go and despatch the company of the Fire.'

He will say, 'At Your service. All good is in Your hands, O Lord! What is the company of the Fire?'

Then He will reply, 'Of every thousand, nine hundred and ninety-nine.'"

The Prophet said, *"On that day the child will become white-haired and every pregnant woman will abort the contents of her womb and you will think people drunk although they are not drunk; but the punishment of Allah is so severe."*

They asked, "Who will be that one?"

The Messenger of Allah, may Allah bless him and grant him peace, replied "Nine hundred and ninety-nine from Yajuj and Majuj, and one from you."

Those present said, "Allah is Greater!"

The Messenger of Allah, may Allah bless him and grant him peace, asked, "Are you not satisfied that you will comprise a quarter of the people of the Garden? By Allah, I hope that you will comprise a quarter of the people of the Garden. By Allah, I hope that you will comprise a third of the people of the Garden. By Allah, I hope that you will comprise half of the people of the Garden!" The people said, "Allah is Greater!" The Messenger of Allah, may Allah bless him and grant him peace, will say: "Amidst all people you represent only one white hair on a black bull, or one black hair on a white bull."[1]

'A'isha said, "I asked, 'Messenger of Allah, will a lover remember the one he loves on the Day of Rising?'"

---

1. Ahmad ibn Hanbal, al-Bukhari and Muslim from Abu Sa'id al-Khudri.

He replied, "'A'isha, there are three places where he will not: at the Balance until he knows whether it is heavy or light; when the books [of actions] are distributed and he is given it in his right or left hand; and when a column of the Fire surrounds them and seethes at them says: 'You trusted in three. You trusted in three. You trusted in three. You trusted in someone who claimed there was another god besides Allah. You trusted in someone who did not believe in the Day of Reckoning. You trusted in any obdurate tyrant.'" He said, "It will surround them and cast them into the depths of Jahannam. Jahannam has a bridge finer than a hair and sharper than a sword which has hooks and spikes on it to grab anyone Allah wishes. People will cross over it like lightning or like the blinking of an eye, like the wind, or like running horses and camels while the angels are saying, 'O Lord, grant safety! Grant safety!' A Muslim who is scratched will be safe but anyone hooked will be upon his face in the Fire." (Ahmad ibn Hanbal)

Every arrogant unbeliever will enter the Fire before the Reckoning – that is, those who arrogantly overstepped Allah's limits, spreading corruption on the earth and committing the most heinous crimes. Their lower selves ordered them to do evil and the lower self contains nothing but evil – evil in its most atrocious forms. They did no good to anything but instead wronged people grievously, torturing them, destroying their homes, making their life a hell. Even if such people were to be returned to this world after the intensity of their sufferings in the Fire of Jahannam they still would not learn the lesson; they would simply revert to their crimes.

Al-Bukhari relates that the Prophet said, may Allah bless him and grant him peace: "The person with the worst punishment on the Day of Rising will be the harshest of them in punishing people in this world."[1]

1. Al-Bukhari, in *at-Tarikh*. Khalid ibn Hakim ibn Hikam reported that Abu 'Ubayda grabbed an Armenian man and Khalid ibn al-Walid spoke to him. They said, "Will you anger the amir?" He said, "I do not want to anger him. I heard the Prophet, may Allah bless him and grant him peace, say..."

Muslim has a similar *hadith* from Hisham ibn Hakim ibn Hizam, who passed by some Nabatean peasants who had been made to stand in the sun and asked, "What is this?" They said, "They are being held on account of the *jizya*." Hisham said, "I testify that I heard the Messenger of Allah say, may Allah bless him and

167

The Prophet said, may Allah bless him and grant him peace: "A bad person is one who is haughty and transgresses and forgets the All-High Compeller. A bad person is one who is haughty and arrogant and forgets the All-Exalted, All-Great. A bad person is one who is aware but then forgets and fails to remember the graves and affliction. A bad person is one who wealthy and then covets and forgets the beginning and the end."

Thabit reported that the Prophet was asked, "Messenger of Allah, how great is the pride of son-and-so!" He replied, "Will it not be followed by death?"

He prayed, may Allah bless him and grant him peace: "O Allah, I seek refuge with You from the overweening nature of pride."

He also said, "Anyone whose soul leaves his body when he is free of three things will enter the Garden: pride, debts and misappropriation."

Abu Bakr as-Siddiq, may Allah be pleased with him, said, "No Muslim should disdain another Muslim. A small Muslim is great in the sight of Allah."

Wahb said, "When Allah created the Garden of Eden, He looked at it and said, 'You are unlawful for any arrogant person.'"

Sulayman was asked about an evil which prevents a good action from being beneficial. He replied: "Pride."

Abu Hurayra reported that the Prophet, may Allah bless him and grant him peace, said, "The tyrants and the arrogant will be gathered on the Day of Rising in the form of specks of dust on which people will tread, because they disdained Allah."

Allah has more tenderness for His creation than a mother for her child; and He thanks His creation for their belief and their being guided to the Straight Path. He Who guides them also gives them the greatest reward and honour. So what is wrong with creatures? Why do they reject and disbelieve? Why are they arrogant and excessive? Allah does not punish His creation out of the desire to punish them or to display His authority or power. Allah is far exalted above that. He punishes them as just repayment for their

---

grant him peace: 'Allah Almighty will punish those who torture people in this world.'"

rejection and disbelief and as just repayment for their oppression and tyranny.

"Why should Allah punish you if you are thankful and believe? Allah is All-Thankful, All-Knowing." (4:147)

Part of Allah's mercy to His servants is that He did not only make a covenant with the descendants of Adam before they came into the world but also renewed it for them during their lives on earth, only punishing them after sending Messengers to them to remind them and warn them. Whoever was not guided after that has the punishment carried out on him.

"Anyone who is rightly guided is guided only to his own benefit. Anyone who is misguided is misguided only to his own detriment. No bearer of a burden can bear another's burden. We never punish before We have sent a Messenger." (17:15)

Allah will repay believers for their good actions with good in this world and the Next World. He will repay unbelievers for their good actions with good in this world alone so that they arrive in the Next World with no good action and are thrown into the Fire. The Fire has degrees which correspond to the degrees of evil actions.

Allah will efface the evil actions of believers through the affliction they suffer in this world. If they are steadfast and thankful in the face of affliction their belief is strong and their evil actions will be effaced and they will enter the Garden. Allah may also purify the bad actions of a Muslim by making their death hard, or in the punishment of the Interspace; or He may expiate the evil actions of believers through their encountering the terrors of the Day of Rising. Believers who were rebellious or who committed grave wrong actions will enter the Fire until they are completely purified of their sins and then they will enter the Garden; but Allah will repay the evil actions of unbelievers with evil in this world and the Next.

169

Anas, may Allah be pleased with him, stated: "When an unbeliever does a good action, he is provided for through it in this world. In the case of a believer, Allah Almighty stores up his good actions for him in this world and follows it up with provision in this world according to how much he obeyed Him."

In a variant reported by Muslim: "Allah does not wrong a Muslim for a good action. He is provided for through it in this world and recompensed for it in the Next World. An unbeliever is provided for by the good actions he did in this world until he reaches the Next World with no good action to be recompensed."

"Do not consider Allah to be heedless of what the wrongdoers do. He is merely deferring them to a Day on which their sight will be transfixed, rushing headlong - heads back, eyes vacant, hearts hollow. Warn mankind of the Day when the punishment will reach them. Those who did wrong will say, 'Our Lord, give us a short reprieve. We will respond to Your call and follow the Messengers.' 'But did you not swear before that you would never meet your downfall?'" (14:42-44)

The *Hawd*: the Pool of the Prophet

"Truly We have given you Kawthar" (108:1)

Allah's creation will emerge from their graves thirsty and will be gathered in a fearful crush. The events on the Day of Gathering will unfold and that Day will be interminably long. People's grief during it will be immeasurable. They will be excruciatingly thirsty. Their feeling of deprivation will increase and the heat will be extreme. Lips will be dry, tongues parched, and faces sad and dejected. People will crave just one drop of water, just one breath of air, just one glimmer of light. They will wish they could shout, weep, or call out, "What is happening!" or "If only I were nothing!"

But circumstances will suddenly change and the mercy of Allah will descend on His pious servants. It will descend with its verdant shade to assuage their hearts with refreshment, sweetness and cool moistness. The terrors will vanish and a fragrance will waft out from the Garden, permeating everywhere. Faces will shine and joy will cover them. Smiles will broaden further when people hear the rippling of water. They will be refreshed by gentle breezes. They will marvel, whispering to one another and questioning one another. They will recognise that it is that abundant bounteousness by which the All-Merciful is generous to His pious servants.

That bounteousness is Kawthar. Kawthar is a river in the Garden which flows into the Pool of the Prophet, may Allah bless him and grant him peace, in the Arena of the Determination. The name Kawthar is also given to the Pool of the Prophet because its source is the river of Kawthar.

According to Muslim, Abu Dharr, may Allah be pleased with him, reported: "I asked, 'Messenger of Allah, what are the vessels of the Pool like?' He replied, 'By the One who holds the soul of Muhammad in His hand, its vessels are more numerous than the

171

stars in the sky on a dark, cloudless night. Whoever drinks from the vessels of the Garden will never thirst again. At its head streams from the Garden flow into it. Whoever drinks from it will never thirst again. It is as wide as it is long, the same as the distance from Oman to Ayla. Its water is whiter than snow and sweeter than honey."

Imam Ahmad related from Anas that he recited the *ayat*, *"Truly We have given you Kawthar"* (108:1) and then declared, "The Messenger of Allah, may Allah bless him and grant him peace, said, 'I have been granted Kawthar. It is a flowing river which does not form a valley. Its banks are mounds of pearls. I struck its earth with my hand and it was pungent musk. Its pebbles are pearls.'" The Pool will appear before all, shimmering and shining with light – the light streaming from myriad precious stones of all shapes and types. The bottom of the Pool and its banks are not of mud and earth, nor of sand and pebbles. The water flows over gems. It flows over pearls and coral, rubies and emeralds, gold and silver. The water of the Pool is whiter than milk, colder than snow, sweeter than honey. Its fragrance is sweeter than musk and amber. How wonderful is the Pool and its water! How beautiful and abundant are its vessels!

Whoever drinks from the water of the Pool will never thirst again. The thirst of those who do not drink from it will never be quenched. No unbeliever will drink from it. The thirsty souls will yearn for a drink of water and people will hasten to the Pool, but they will find someone already there before them who will call them and invite them to drink. They will be amazed and astonished. They will see him clearly right in front of them. They will meet him face to face. It is Muhammad, peace and blessings be upon him! The cries will go up: "O beloved! O beloved! O Muhammad! O Beloved of Allah!" Tears of joy will flow down their cheeks. Finally they will meet Muhammad and with him they will meet Abu Bakr, 'Umar, 'Uthman, 'Ali, and the other noble Companions.

There are many pools there, shimmering with light. They are the Lights of all the Prophets, peace be upon them. That one is Ibrahim, may Allah bless him and grant him peace, and that one is

Musa. Also present are 'Isa, Nuh, Sulayman, and all the noble Prophets of Allah. Every Prophet has a pool from which the believers of his Community will drink and which will be denied to unbelievers. The souls of those who believed in the Messengers and Prophets of Allah will yearn to meet them. So the meeting will be one of joy and longing, of delight and yearning, encompassing every generation throughout time.

Anas ibn Malik reported that the Messenger of Allah, may Allah bless him and grant him peace, said. "My Pool is such-and-such a size and in it are vessels as numerous as the stars. It is sweeter than honey and cooler than snow and whiter than milk. Whoever drinks from it will never thirst. Whoever does not drink from it will never be quenched."

According to Salman, may Allah be pleased with him, "The Messenger of Allah, may Allah bless him and grant him peace, spoke to us on the last day of Sha'ban and declared, "O people! A great and blessed month is in front of you," and he mentioned the entire *hadith* about the excellence of the month of Ramadan until he said, "Whoever satisfies someone fasting in it, Allah will let him drink a drink from my Pool after which he will not thirst until he enters the Garden." (Abu Bakr ibn Khuzayma)

Many *hadiths* have been reported about the Pool and its appearance. The Messenger of Allah, may Allah bless him and grant him peace, said, "I have a Pool whose length is as great as the distance from the Ka'ba to Jerusalem." In another, "Its width is as great as the distance from Oman to Ayla." Ayla is at the top of the Gulf of Aqaba on the Red Sea. It was once a flourishing city but is now in ruins. On other occasions, the Prophet, peace and blessings be upon him, reckoned the dimensions of the Pool by time: "My Pool is a month's journey round." All of these distances come to the same thing. What is meant by them is that the Pool is very extensive and that he, may Allah bless him and grant him peace, addressed each group of people using the sort of distances they were familiar with.

We can add to the noble hadiths we have already mentioned what al-Bukhari transmitted from 'Abdullah ibn 'Amr ibn al-'As: "The Messenger of Allah, may Allah bless him and grant him

173

peace, said, 'My Pool is a month's journey round and its sides are equal. Its water is whiter than silver and its fragrance is sweeter than musk. Its jugs are like the stars of the sky. Whoever comes and drinks from it will never thirst again afterwards."

The Prophet, may Allah bless him and grant him peace, will precede his Community to the Pool. He will recognise it as each Prophet of a Community will recognise the water particular to them. The Community of Muhammad will be distinguished by the light of *wudu'* since light will shine from their faces and the limbs which water touched during *wudu'*. The Prophet will see some men of his Community, whom the angels suddenly drive away from the Pool. He will call out, "O Lord! My companions!" He will be told, "You do not know what they did after you. They reverted and committed acts of disobedience."

Al-Bukhari transmitted from 'Abdullah, may Allah be pleased with him, that the Prophet said, may Allah bless him and grant him peace: "I will come first to the Pool, and some of your men will appear before me and then be taken away from me. I will say, "O Lord, my companions!" It will be said, "You do not know what they introduced after your lifetime."

Ibn 'Abbas said, "The Messenger of Allah, may Allah bless him and grant him peace, was asked about standing before the Lord of the Worlds and whether there would be any water there. He replied, 'By the One who holds my soul in His hand, there is water there. The friends of Allah will drink from the Pools of the Prophets and Allah will send seventy thousand angels with ropes of fire in their hands to drive the unbelievers away from the Pools of the Prophets.'"

Al-Hakim at-Tirmidhi transmitted in *Nawadir al-Usul* from a *hadith* narrated by 'Uthman ibn Maz'un that the Prophet, may Allah bless him and grant him peace, said at the end of it, "O 'Uthman, do not turn away from my *Sunna*. If anyone turns away from my *Sunna* and then dies before repenting, the angels will beat his face, driving him away from my Pool on the Day of Resurrection."

Abu Talut al-'Anbari said that he heard his father Barza report, "I heard the Messenger of Allah, may Allah bless him and grant

174

him peace, say about the Pool: 'If anyone denies me, Allah will not let him drink from it.'" (Ibn Abi Dunya)

According to Abu Sa'id, the Messenger of Allah, may Allah bless him and grant him peace, said, "I have a Pool whose length is like the distance between the Ka'ba and Jerusalem and whose water is whiter than milk. Its vessels are as numerous as the stars. Every Prophet will call his community and every Prophet will have a Pool. Some of them will come to it in their hundreds, some will come to it in troops, some will come to it in groups, some will come in ones and twos, and some will come to it all alone.' They will be told, 'You have arrived.' I will be the Prophet will the most followers on the Day of Rising." (Ibn Abi Dunya)

According to Ibn Majah, Abu Sa'id al-Khudri, may Allah be pleased with him, reported that the Prophet, may Allah bless him and grant him peace, said, "I have a Pool which extends as far as the distance between the Ka'ba and Jerusalem, whose water is whiter than milk. Its vessels are as numerous as the stars. And I will be the Prophet with the most followers on the Day of Rising."

According to Ibn Majah, as-Sunabaji al-Ahmasi reported that the Messenger of Allah, may Allah bless him and grant him peace, said, "I will be the first of you to reach the Pool and through you I will have the most numerous Community, so do not fight one another after my lifetime."

Ibn 'Umar reported that the Messenger of Allah, may Allah bless him and grant him peace, said, "Kawthar is a river in the Garden whose banks are made of gold and whose water flows over pearls. Its water is whiter than milk and sweeter than honey." (Imam Ahmad)

The gifts of Allah are bountiful and without any limits. Devote yourself sincerely to your Lord. Be sincere with Him in the obligatory prayer and in the voluntary. Do not associate anyone with Him. Rather be thankful for His blessing. Sacrifice - offer animals in sacrifice out of gratitude.

*"Truly We have given you the Great Abundance (*Kawthar*), so pray to your Lord and sacrifice."*
(108:1-2)

In the *Musnad* of Imam Ahmad, the Prophet, may Allah bless him and grant him peace, is reported to have said, "There is no day on which the sea does not ask its Lord for permission to drown the son of Adam and on which the angels do not ask His permission to hasten his destruction. The Almighty Lord says, 'Leave My slave. I have more knowledge of him since I originated him from the earth. If he were your slave, he would be your concern. Since he is My slave, he is from Me and to Me. By My might and My majesty, if My slave comes to Me in the night, I accept him. If he comes to Me in the day, I accept him. If he draws near to Me a cubit, I draw near him a span. If he draws near Me a span, I draw near him two spans. If he walks to Me, I run to him. If he asks My forgiveness, I forgive him. If he asks Me to overlook, I overlook. If he turns to Me in repentance, I turn to him. Who has greater generosity and magnanimity than I? I am the Ever-Generous, the Munificent. My slaves go to bed having committed enormities and yet I preserve them and protect them in their beds.

"If anyone advances to Me, I meet him. If anyone abandons something for My sake, I give to him beyond measure. If anyone acts by My strength and power, I make iron soft for him. If anyone wants what I want, I want what he wants. The people of remembrance are the people who sit with Me. The people who show thanks to Me are the people to whom I give increase. The people who obey Me are the people who receive My generosity. As for the people who disobey Me, I do not make them despair. If they turn to Me in repentance, I am their Beloved. If they do not turn, I am their physician. I test them with afflictions in order to purify them of faults.'"

Two Paradigms for Emulation

"Which is better: one who founds his building on fear of Allah and His good pleasure, or one who founds his building on the edge of a crumbling cliff so that it collapses with him into the Fire of Hell? Allah does not love people who are wrongdoers."

(9:109)

"Anyone who has been given wisdom has been given great good. But no one remembers except people of intelligence." (2:269)

Ibrahim ibn Adham

A man came to Ibrahim ibn Adham, may Allah be pleased with him, and said, "Abu Ishaq, I am unable to control my lower self. Please give me something to help me with it."

"If you accept five conditions," said Ibrahim, "and are able to put them into practice, your disobedience will not cause you any problem."

"Just tell me what they are, Abu Ishaq!" the man said.

"The first is that when you want to disobey Allah you do not eat anything He provides."

"Then how will I get anything to eat? Everything on the earth is from Him!"

"So is it right to eat His provision and disobey Him at the same time?" replied Ibrahim.

"No, it is not. What is the second condition?"

"When you want to disobey Him, move off His land."

"That is even more difficult!" exclaimed the man. "In that case where will I live?"

"Is it right to eat His provision and live on His land and then to disobey Him?" asked Ibrahim.

"No, it is not," replied the man. "What is the third condition?"

"When you want to disobey Him in spite of eating His provision and living on His land, find a place where He will not see you and disobey Him there."

"What do you mean, Ibrahim? He knows everything that happens even in the most hidden places!"

"So is it right to disobey Him when you eat His provision and live on His land and when you know that He can see everything you do?"

"It certainly is not!" the man replied. "Tell me the fourth condition."

"That when the Angel of Death arrives to take your soul, you say to him, 'Give me a reprieve so that I can repent and act righteously for Allah.'"

"But he won't listen to me!"

"Then if you cannot ward off death long enough to give yourself time to repent, and you know that when it comes there will be no reprieve, how can you hope to be saved?"

"What is the fifth?"

"That when the angels of the Fire come to you to take you to the Fire, you do not go with them."

"They will take me whether I like it or not!" exclaimed the man.

"So how can you hope to be saved?"

"Enough, enough, Ibrahim! I ask Allah's forgiveness and I turn to Him!"

The man's repentance was sincere and from that time on he was assiduous in his worship and avoided acts of disobedience until the day he died.

Hatim al-Asamm

It is related that one day Shaqiq al-Balkhi asked his student Hatim al-Asamm, "How long have you kept my company?"

"Thirty-three years," he replied.

"And what have you learned from me in all this time?"

"Eight things," he said.

"We belong to Allah and we return to Him!" exclaimed Shaqiq. "You have spent your whole life with me and only learned eight things! What are they?"

"Firstly," replied Hatim, "I looked at mankind and I saw that everyone loves something and continues to do so. When he goes to his grave, whatever he loved leaves him. Therefore I made my good actions what I love, for when I enter the grave they will enter it along with me."

"You have done well," said Shaqiq. "What is the second?"

"The second is that I examined the words of the Almighty, *'But as for him who feared the Station of his Lord and forbade the self its appetites, the Garden shall be his refuge.'* (79:40-41) Knowing that the words of the Almighty are true, I strove against myself to keep my appetites at bay until I was firm in obeying Allah Almighty.

"The third is that I looked at people and saw that everyone has something of worth which they value and protect. Then I looked at the words of the Almighty, *'What is with you comes to an end. But what is with Allah is everlasting.'* (16:96) So whenever something of value comes to me, I direct it to Allah Almighty so that it may remain with Him for me.

"The fourth is that I looked at Allah's creatures and saw that all of them set much store by property, reputation, honour, and lineage. I examined those things and found them to be nothing. Then I looked at the words of the Almighty, *'The noblest among you in Allah's sight is the most godfearing of you.'* (49:13) So I set much store by fear of Allah so that I might be noble in His sight.

179

"The fifth is that I looked at people and I found that some of them attacked others and some of them cursed others; and I realised that the reason they did that was envy. Then I looked at the words of the Almighty, *'We have meted out among them their livelihood in the life of this world.'* (43:32) So I abandoned envy and enmity towards creation, knowing that what is allotted to me will and must reach me.

"The sixth is that I saw that people fought and were hostile to one another. I looked for my true enemy and found it to be Shaytan and indeed Allah Almighty says, *'Shaytan is an enemy to you, so treat him as an enemy.'* (35:6) So I made him my enemy and loved everyone else.

"The seventh is that I looked at mankind and found them seeking excessive wealth and abasing themselves because of it. I looked at the words of the Almighty, *'There is no creature on the earth whose provision is not with Allah alone.'* (11:6) I realised that I am one of those who are provided for and so I busied myself with Allah Almighty and abandoned everything besides Him.

"The eighth is that I looked at people and I saw that they relied on different things: one on his commerce, another on his profession, and yet another on his health. Every creature was relying on another creature! I looked at the words of the Almighty, *'And whoever puts his trust in Allah, He is enough for him.'* (65:3) Therefore I put my trust in Allah Almighty."

"Hatim," said Shaqiq, "Allah has given you success, and you have left nothing out. *'He gives wisdom to whomever He wishes.'*"

"We did not create the heaven and the earth and everything between them to no purpose. That is the opinion of those who reject. So woe to those who reject, on account of the Fire! Shall We make those who believe and perform right actions the same as those who cause corruption in the earth? Shall We make the godfearing the same as the dissolute? A blessed Book We have sent down to you. Therefore let people possessing understanding ponder its Signs and be reminded." (38:27-29)

Bibliography

al-Ahadith al-Qudsiyya

al-Ghazzali, Abu Hamid Muhammad ibn Muhammad, *Ihya' 'Ulum ad-Din*

____, *Mukashafat al-Qulub al-Muqarriba ila hadrat 'Allam al-Ghuyub*

Ibn al-Athir, 'Ali ibn Muhammad, *al-Kamil fi't-Tarikh*

Ibn Hajar al-'Asqallani, Ahmad ibn 'Ali, *Fath al-Bari bi-sharh Sahih al-Bukhari*

Ibn Hisham, Abu Muhammad 'Abdu'l-Malik, *Sirat an-Nabi*

Ibn Kathir, Isma'il ibn 'Umar, *Tafsir al-Qur'an al-'Adhim*

____, *Nihaya al-Bidaya wa'n-nihaya*, ed. Isma'il ibn Muhammad al-Ansari

Ibn Qayyim al-Jawziyya, Muhammad ibn Abi Bakr, *Madarij as-Salikin bayna manazil 'iyyaka na'budu wa iyyaka nasta'in'*

____, *Zad al-Ma'ad fi huda khayr al-'ubbad*

Khalid, Muhammad, *Rijal hawl ar-Rasul*

Mahmud, Mustafa, *al-Qur'an: Muhawala fi-fahm 'asri*

al-Mawsu'a al-'Ilimiyya

Makhluf, Husaynayn Muhammad, *Kalimat al-Qur'an*

Muhammad Fu'ad 'Abdu'l-Baqi, *Al-Mu'jam al-Mufahras li-alfaz al-Qur'an al-Karim*

Muhammad al-Hajjar, *Samir al-Mu'minin*

al-Muhasibi, al-Harith ibn Asad, *at-Tawahhum*

Al-Muntakhab fi Tafsir al-Qur'an

An-Nawawi, *Riyad as-Salihin*

al-Qurtubi, Muhammad ibn Ahmad, *at-Tadhkira fi Ahwal al-mawta wa umur al-akhira*

___, *Yawm al-faz' al-akbar*

Qutb, Sayyid, *Fi zilal al-Qur'an*

ar-Razi, Muhammad ibn Abi Bakr, *Mukhtar as-sihah*

ash-Sha'rawi, Muhammad Mitwalli., *Yawm al-qiyama*